BEST OF
FOOD
BLOGS
COOKBOOK

Foodista

100 Great Recipes, Photographs, and Voices

BEST OF FOOD BLOGS COOKBOOK

**Edited by Sheri L. Wetherell,
Barnaby Dorfman, and Colin M. Saunders**

**Andrews McMeel
Publishing, LLC**

Kansas City • Sydney • London

10 11 12 13 14 RR3 10 9 8 7 6 5 4 3 2 1

ISBN: 978-0-7407-9767-5

Library of Congress Control Number: 2010924502

www.andrewsmcmeel.com
www.foodista.com

Book design by Diane Marsh

ATTENTION: SCHOOLS AND BUSINESSES
Andrews McMeel books are available at quantity discounts with bulk purchase for educational, business, or sales promotional use. For information, please write to: Special Sales Department, Andrews McMeel Publishing, LLC, 1130 Walnut Street, Kansas City, Missouri 64106.

This book is for all the food
bloggers and home cooks
of the world. Your passion
inspires us and we thank you.

Contents

ACKNOWLEDGMENTS

This book would not be possible without all the wonderful food bloggers who submitted recipes, blog posts, and photography. Whether you made it into the book or not, you are all winners to us. Your creativity and passion inspire us, and we thank you from the bottom of our hearts (and stomachs!).

And thanks to the Foodista community for casting your votes! We took your lead on what you thought was great and from these, narrowed it to the final 100, truly making this a community project.

We'd also like to give humongous thanks to our incredible Foodista team for all their hard work on compiling this cookbook. They all got in the trenches and went above and beyond, even without bribes of beer and pizza. We are truly blessed to have such a team. Our fabulous and uber-smart partner and chief technology officer, Colin Saunders, who hates the word "pants" and says "water" like a true Englishman should (even though he's only half English); our lead engineer, Jesse Dawson, whose name sounds like he should be slinging guns in a western but who instead fires off code faster than any cowboy could; our graphic designer, Karlyn Oyama, who makes not only beautiful designs for us but also delicious marshmallow treat birthday cakes and other yummies; our community developer, Melissa Peterman, a bright ray of sunshine who also happens to be an exceptional cook with an unwavering passion for food and cooking; our social media intern, Helen Pitlick, a fabulous girl and the only vegan we've ever known who loves to write about bacon; our data-mining intern, Patrick Mullen, for adding up all the votes; and our editorial interns, Kate Opatz and Carolyn (Carrie) Barr, who helped carefully review every submission. And our incredible interns and contractors: Aaron Krill, Alisa Escanlar, Andrea Mitchell, Anneka Gerhardt, Desiree Lowe, Jeff Kahn, Kailash Thakur, Sarah Donnell, Sergio Alvarez, and Taylor Davies.

Big thanks are also due to Kirsty Melville at Andrews McMeel for being so sold on the idea of this book and embracing food blogging and technology as we've seen no other publisher do. We love you! And, to our wonderful editor, Jean Lucas, for her guidance and patience.

Many thanks to Dianne Jacob, who authored the first book we read on food writing and, as fate would have it, became an editor on this book. Never did we imagine that happening, and we were thrilled! Through her wisdom we have learned a great deal about recipe writing. We thank you for your help on the book, but also for guiding bloggers in the art and business of food writing.

We couldn't have done this book or developed Foodista.com without the support of many. Our parents—Kathy and Greg Roduner, Rich and Dreama Wetherell, Mandy Evans, Ron and Betsy Dorfman, and Christopher and Carla Saunders. Our friends and advisors—Tracy Sarich and John Chase, Amy Pennington, Kathleen Flinn, Kim Ricketts, and Warren Etheridge. The great folks at Amazon.com who believed in us—Jorrit Van der Meulen, Matt Peterson, Jeff Blackburn, Peter Krawiec, and Jeff Bezos.

Last, but certainly not least, I would like to personally thank Barnaby Dorfman, my partner in business and life, for his tireless work on both this cookbook and our many Foodista projects. Your tenacity is both awe inspiring and amazing to watch. Words cannot express my gratitude.

—SHERI L. WETHERELL,
FOUNDER AND V.P., EDITORIAL

Introduction

It's nothing short of an act of love (or addiction!) to develop, photograph, and share dishes you create in your home with the world. Many of us do this daily through our food blogs, and it is indeed an art to be appreciated. A year prior to launching Foodista.com in December of 2008 we started our own food blog. Food blogging was a new world to us and became our way of connecting with the online food community—a tool from which to learn and be inspired by an impassioned culture of food.

We quickly discovered that the tight-knit online community of bloggers also hungered to connect offline. Sharing a common dream to take their "home art" to the next level, we created the International Food Blogger Conference (IFBC), an event focused on food, technology, and writing. From that first conference in May of 2009 we had an "aha" moment with one of our publishing speakers, Kirsty Melville. Why not put together a collection of interesting voices, recipes, and photography in a blogger cookbook?

To get started, we announced the Foodista Best of Food Blogs Cookbook contest and received more than 1,500 entries in just three months. We relied on the Foodista community to cast their votes, and then we selected from their top choices. So this cookbook is clearly a user-generated piece of work. Narrowing the top-rated recipes down to a final 100 was still no easy feat!

The first happy surprise was the number of international submissions. Indeed, we share a common thread as the world clearly has a passion for food. We received entries from Brazil, Turkey, Dubai, India, all across Asia, an expanse of Europe, Canada—more than twenty countries in all. From their stories we learned about new foods (hallabong?), enjoyed memories of family, and read about celebrations of adopting a child, living life as an expat in a new country, a child catching a huge salmon on a toy rod . . .

The stories made us weep, laugh hysterically, and simply made us want to hang out with the authors. This is what we love about food blogs and the writers who take the time to document their experiences and recipes on the Web. More than any other type of food writing, food blogging gives us intimate snapshots of a diversity of lives and kitchens. This unabashed writing and cooking from heart and soul is a truly new art form built on a rapidly evolving platform of technologies.

Central to this book is an experiment in bridging the worlds of traditional print publishing and the new media of blogs. We'd like to note that not all of these dishes went through a traditional recipe testing process, but rather were produced in the homes of seasoned cooks who have built online audiences for their unique creations. We trust good home cooking, just as we would if we asked for the recipe a friend had just made us for dinner. We have standardized much of the presentation, especially of quantities, measures, and ingredients, but wherever possible we strived to preserve the original voice of the blogger. Finally, many entries are family recipes, and we felt we shouldn't mess with tradition!

ABOUT THE EDITORS

Sheri L. Wetherell
Founder and Vice President, Editorial

Sheri grew up surrounded by food on both sides of her family. Her paternal grandmother owned a diner for many years, and her maternal grandmother (mother of five daughters) was always found in the kitchen baking or whipping up garden-fresh tomato juice. Her mother instilled in her the importance of healthy, wholesome eating and fed the family homemade soups, breads, and fresh carrot juice. Through her grandmothers, mother, and numerous travels overseas, Sheri developed her love of food. She honed her palate and taste for travel by hopping planes with her airline pilot father, spent nearly a year studying in Italy and traveling in Greece, and taught English in Tokyo for three years. Her professional background is in traditional and online marketing, where she worked for companies such as Amazon.com, Microsoft, Nordstrom, and eBay. With Foodista.com she has finally found her true passion—immersion in the world of food.

Barnaby Dorfman
Founder and Chief Executive Officer

A native New Yorker, Barnaby's family introduced him to variety in food and culture, which grew into a passion during years of living in and traveling throughout Mexico, Spain, and Italy. Barnaby's first professional cooking was done in high school at a resort in New York's Catskill Mountains. Later he cooked for Taste Catering in San Francisco during college at California State University. A serial entrepreneur, Barnaby's first start-up was Marsee Baking, the first all-scratch, European-style bakery group in Portland, Oregon. He left the world of baking for an MBA at Dartmouth College and since 1996 has worked in technology management at various start-ups, Microsoft, and Amazon.com. Barnaby's fifth start-up, Foodista.com, offers the opportunity to combine lifelong loves of cooking and technology.

Colin M. Saunders
Founder and Chief Technology Officer

Lucky enough to be born into one of Napa Valley's oldest family wine estates, Trefethen Family Vineyards, Colin has been surrounded by a love of good food, good wine, and hard work since he was a babe in arms. He rolled out pie dough on a cold table with his mother in San Francisco, brewed beer at Berkeley in Oenology 101, and played the ponies with his econometrics professor at Golden Gate Fields. His true love, however, is writing code. Colin has been flipping bits since 1985, working at Microsoft, Amazon.com, and several start-ups along the way. At Foodista.com, Colin is happy to be also flipping pancakes.

Foodista, Inc.

Based in Seattle, Washington, the technology company operates Foodista.com, the online cooking encyclopedia everyone can edit. This collaborative project leverages open-source software, cloud computing resources, and wisdom of the crowds to rapidly develop cooking software and content. The company is funded by private investors and Amazon.

1 Cocktails and Appetizers

CHANTERELLE MUSHROOMS WITH BLUE CHEESE PIE

CUCUMBER MINT TEA SANDWICHES

DOUBLE-CHEESE SOUFFLÉ WITH SPICED PEAR

FATTEH WITH YOGURT AND PINE NUTS

GEODUCK CEVICHE

GLUTEN-FREE VEGETARIAN SPRING ROLLS
  WITH THAI-STYLE PEANUT SAUCE

LOTUS ROOT CHIPS WITH TOASTED NORI-SESAME SALT

LOVAGE SPRITZERS

MUMMY JUICE

MARTINI PUFFS

OKRACOKE CLAMS CASINO

PROSCIUTTO-WRAPPED BROCCOLINI WITH BASIL CRISPS

NEER MOR SPICED BUTTERMILK

SCALLOP SANDWICHES

TAWNY MANHATTAN

SEATTLE FOOD GEEK'S BROILED HONEY-GLAZED SPICED FIGS

VEGETARIAN CALIFORNIA ROLLS

VEGETARIAN SCOTCH EGGS

Chanterelle Mushrooms with Blue Cheese Pie

SIMONE VAN DEN BERG
ALMERE, NETHERLANDS
JUNGLEFROG COOKING
http://junglefrog-cooking.com/chanterelles-tart

I am a photographer from the Netherlands who—obviously—loves to cook! I've always really liked cooking, but since I discovered the world of food blogging it has become so much more fun. What better way to learn than by reading other people's blogs from around the world, competing in challenges and so on?

SERVES 4

I was so happy when we went to the farmers' market in Amsterdam on Saturday to find an entire stall filled with all sorts of mushrooms. Remember that in the supermarkets here you can only ever find button mushrooms, chestnut mushrooms, and the occasional oyster mushroom and shiitake if you're really lucky. But I had never even seen chanterelles, let alone eaten them fresh, so I was quite excited when we found them in the market. I wanted to make these into an appetizer for when my friend would come over for dinner Tuesday, and Olga came up with the suggestion of making them into a tart with puff pastry. This reminded me I still had puff pastry in the freezer, so that would be perfect to make some quick appetizers for dinner. Because I wanted to try out the flavors, I made a little one in the afternoon with chestnut mushrooms and the cheese I bought, and it was delicious. And it is really almost too simple to throw together and looks quite good and tastes fantastic. You can of course use any kind of mushroom you want with this, but the chanterelles were very tasty. In the Netherlands puff pastry is sold in little square packets with separate sheets about 10 to 15 centimeters square and already thin enough to use as they are, ideal for these little pies.

I also made a version with little pomodori tomatoes, which worked very well too. It's a little less strong in taste, and I prefer the flavors of the chanterelle-only version, but of course you could make endless variations with this.

7 ounces chanterelle mushrooms

1½ teaspoons olive oil

Salt and pepper

1 sheet puff pastry

3 ounces blue cheese

1¾ ounces pecorino cheese, grated

1 egg, beaten

1 Preheat the oven to 400°F.

2 Cut the chanterelles into manageable sizes. Keep in mind they need to fit on top of the puff pastry and you don't want huge chunks here, but not too small either. Toss the mushrooms in a bowl with the olive oil and salt and pepper to taste.

3 On a lightly floured work surface, roll out the puff pastry (defrosted, of course, if frozen) just enough to create a square. Then cut into 4 squares. Put some of the mushrooms in the middle, being sure to leave the sides free. Don't be too shy. You want to have a nice little pile of mushrooms there. They will decrease in size in the oven.

4 Generously add little chunks of the blue cheese here and there. Make sure to have an even distribution of cheesy goodness. Sprinkle grated pecorino cheese on top of each pie.

5 Brush some of the beaten egg on the sides of the puff pastry and fold it creatively into a little basket so the cheese stays in when it starts to melt. Plus the corners will become nice and crispy too. Pinch it tightly to make sure it stays put once heated.

6 Put the little pies in the oven for about 12 minutes, then lower the temperature to 350°F and bake for another 15 minutes, until golden brown and crispy. Serve warm or at room temperature.

Cucumber Mint Tea Sandwiches

KATHY PATALSKY
NEW YORK, NEW YORK
HEALTHY. HAPPY. LIFE.
http://kblog.lunchboxbunch.com/2010/02/cucumber-mint-tea-sandwiches-modern-tea.html

I'm the creator of the healthy kids brand The Lunchbox Bunch (LBB). My LBB mission: Turn ordinary kids into healthy eating, kid-chef superstars! Each with a curiosity to taste, love, and learn about a wide variety of fruits and veggies.

MAKES 8 BITES

When I hear the phrase tea and sandwiches, I picture a well-postured group of early-century women in wide pastel-laced hats, nibbling tiny white-bread sandwiches with the crusts sliced off, and shiny orange marmalade slathered inside. Or I picture a little girl giggling in her bedroom, having a tea-free tea party. Perhaps she snatched her mum's silver tea set, sprawled it out on the floor, and invited all her favorite stuffed animals for a few giggles, sips, and plentiful pours of "tea"—aka water from the bathroom sink. But the timeless art of the tea party doesn't have to be stuffy or fit for a five-year-old. It can be modern, delicious—and perhaps even a daily wellness ritual to embrace. Not into tea? Cappuccino will do.

My vegan recipe was inspired by a recipe my mother prepared once when I was a teenager. I remember I was dragged kicking and screaming to another one of my older sister's vocal recitals. It was in a large concert hall downtown, and my mother was signed up to contribute a plate of hors d'oeuvres for the guests. I watched my mother all morning in the kitchen as she stuffed tiny slices of butter, fresh sprigs of mint, and thick crisp slices of cucumber between small, decrusted triangles of white bread. Each tiny sandwich was big enough for one bite—finger sandwiches. The mint smelled so fresh and the cucumber so perfectly cool and crisp. I thought, "How odd to be slicing cold hard butter as a sandwich ingredient"—especially since my mother rarely used butter on anything. But she called the finger sandwiches elegant. I tasted one and loved it. Cucumber, mint, and soft white bread, with an odd creamy bite of butter. Those flavors stay on the tip of my taste buds even today. But nowadays I don't consume dairy, and I wasn't too keen on placing a thick slice of vegan buttery spread in my light and petite tea sandwiches, so I made a few substantial modifications to the classic recipe. I even whipped up my own sweet 'n' spicy wasabi pepper vegan spread in place of butter. Try this recipe on a Saturday afternoon or for a lazy Sunday brunch at home. It's perfect for an afternoon party or springtime picnic in the park. Cool, crisp, refreshing, and supereasy to make, these are sandwiches I will definitely be making again and again.

WASABI MAPLE SPREAD:

2 tablespoons vegan mayonnaise

1 tablespoon maple syrup

2 teaspoons wasabi powder

Dash of black pepper

SANDWICHES:

½ organic cucumber

Fresh mint leaves

Fresh dill

4 slices bread

Black pepper

1 Whip together all the spread ingredients in a small bowl. Thinly slice the cucumbers. You can do thick crunchy slices or thin silky slices—your choice. Gather your fresh herbs, rinse, and pat dry.

2 Spread a very thin layer of the spread on each slice of bread.

3 Layer cucumber slices on top of the spread. Next, add a layer of mint and dill. You can add both herbs to each sandwich or do half dill and half mint. Grind fresh black pepper inside the sandwiches.

4 Close each sandwich and slice into quarter cubes or triangles. Plate and serve.

VARIATION: Add a thin layer of spicy sun-dried tomato spread or a dash of red pepper flakes for an extra spicy kick of flavor. Another pretty addition would be edible flowers—add inside the sandwiches or as an edible garnish to the serving patter.

Double-Cheese Soufflé with Spiced Pear

If you want to test your organisation and time management skills, then make a soufflé. From preparing the cream sauce to whipping the egg whites and serving, perfect timing is the key to the magical soufflé moment! Admire the gorgeous risen puff. Breathe in the aroma of cream cheese and chives floating about your dining room and take in a breath of French air. Spoon through the fluffiness of the magical dish. Close your eyes and let only your taste buds watch the soufflé melt down through your throat. It suddenly makes perfect sense why soufflé is a mouthwatering recipe to die for.

SOUFFLÉ:

1 tablespoon butter, plus more for greasing the dishes

2 tablespoons all-purpose or buckwheat flour

½ cup soy milk

½ cup (4 ounces) chopped goat cheese

5 tablespoons grated Parmesan cheese

1 tablespoon chopped chives

2 eggs, separated

Pinch of salt and pepper

SPICED PEAR:

1 tablespoon honey

½ teaspoon pie spice

1 organic pear, peeled, halved, and cored

JOE DAMRONGPHIWAT
MELBOURNE, VICTORIA, AUSTRALIA
MY DELICIOUS BLOG
http://mydeliciousblog.blogspot.com/2010/02/double-cheese-souffle-with-spiced-pear.html

I was brought up in a family where food is a way of life, not just a source of nutrition. After searching for my niche for years, I finally realised my big dreams: food stylist, food photographer, food writer, boutique patisserie owner, celebrity chef . . . so many opportunities to explore. My Delicious Blog for the moment is my space, a reminder of the possibilities to live my dream.

SERVES 2

1 Preheat the oven to 300°F and grease two 10-ounce soufflé dishes with butter.

2 Melt the butter in a saucepan over low heat, about 1 minute. Stir in the flour and cook for 1 minute. Gradually add the milk. Keep stirring all the time until the sauce is thickened. Continue cooking for 2 minutes.

3 Add the cheeses, chives, and egg yolks. Season with salt and pepper. Remove from the heat.

4 Beat the egg whites until stiff. Fold the whipped egg whites into the cheese mixture in two additions. Spoon the mixture into the prepared dishes. Bake them for 12 minutes—watch them rise!

5 In the meantime, make the spiced pear. Pour the honey into a clean saucepan over low heat. Add the mixed spices. Add the pear and cook on both sides for about 5 minutes. Slice the pears and serve alongside the soufflé.

Fatteh with Yogurt and Pine Nuts

RAJANI
UNITED ARAB EMIRATES
VEGETARIAN IN ME

http://vegetarianinme.
blogspot.com/2008/06/
fatth-with-yoghurt-and-
pine-nuts.html

SERVES 2

1   cup dried chickpeas

2   tablespoons olive oil, plus more for garnish

1   khubus or pita bread, shredded

2   tablespoons pine nuts

     Salt

1   teaspoon ground cumin

1½ cups thick yogurt

1   teaspoon chili powder, for garnish

1 Soak the chickpeas in cold water for 8 hours or overnight. Boil until soft and drain, reserving the liquid.

2 Heat 2 tablespoons of the olive oil in a saucepan and fry the shredded bread until crispy. Remove.

3 In the same pan, toast the pine nuts and set aside.

4 Add salt to taste and the cumin to the yogurt and give the mixture a good whisk. If the yogurt is too thick, dilute it, using the reserved chickpea liquid. Add the chickpeas to the yogurt and give it a final mix.

5 To assemble: Line the bottom of a bowl with the fried bread. Pour the chickpea-yogurt mixture on top.

6 Garnish with a sprinkle of chili powder, toasted pine nuts, and a drizzle of olive oil.

Dining out in UAE's many Arabic/Lebanese joints is not a very bright prospect for vegetarians. First of all, the very idea of being a vegetarian is balked upon! However, having said that, let me also add that vegetarians get to eat (according to me) the tastiest part of Arabic cuisine—the salads and starters. No Arabic meal is complete without lavish portions of greens. The nonvegetarians, so drooly over their approaching kebabs and meat platters, often forget about these yummy bunches of flavour. That's where I strike! The greens along with khubus and a drizzle of olive oil make for a great, fresh nibble. Some of my other favorites are manakish (a bread with cheese stuffing), saj (an open bread with different toppings), hummus, baba ghanoush, lentil soup (I so love lentil soup with a dash of lemon juice), fattoush (a crispy salad), labneh and za'atar, yummy stuffed fatayer, and sticky rice. There are loads more. But here's where I stop for now!

Geoduck Ceviche

LANGDON COOK
SEATTLE, WASHINGTON
FAT OF THE LAND: ADVENTURES OF A 21ST
CENTURY FORAGER
http://fat-of-the-land.blogspot.com/2009/08/duck-hunting.html

I am a writer, editor, forager, and author of *Fat of the Land: Adventures of a 21st Century Forager.*

SERVES 6

Geoducks (pronounced "gooey-ducks") are the world's largest burrowing clams, making their home in coastal waters from California to Alaska. This ceviche highlights their unique taste and texture with a sweet and spicy kick. I like to serve it over a bed of fresh baby greens. Use only the geoduck's neck meat.

NOTE: To clean a live geoduck, immerse it in boiling water for 8 seconds. Now you can pull off the thin sheath that protects the siphon. Slice off the siphon at the base and nip off the last ½ inch or so of the dark tip. This neck meat can be used for sashimi or ceviche. Extract the rest of the clam with a paring knife, cutting the adductor muscles on the inside of the shell. Throw away the bulbous gut and use the remaining meat in a sauté or stir-fry.

1   clove garlic, minced

1   serrano chile, seeded and finely diced

1   tablespoon fish sauce

1   tablespoon brown sugar

1½ limes

½   pound geoduck neck (siphon), thinly sliced

¼   cup diced red onion

¼   cup diced sweet red pepper

½   cup cucumber, peeled and chopped

½   cup peeled, seeded, and chopped papaya

    Handful of cilantro, stemmed and chopped

1   tablespoon sesame seeds, toasted

    Salt

1 Combine the garlic, serrano chile, fish sauce, and brown sugar in a small bowl. Stir with the juice of ½ lime.

2 In a large bowl, cover the sliced geoduck with juice of 1 lime, stir, and let sit for 30 minutes.

3 Add the sauce to the sliced geoduck and then add the onion, red pepper, cucumber, papaya, cilantro, and sesame seeds. Stir and season with salt.

VARIATION: If geoduck clams are not available, you may use razor clams, scallops, butter clams, or any other firm-fleshed shellfish.

Gluten-Free Vegetarian Spring Rolls with Thai-Style Peanut Sauce

CINDE
WASHINGTON
GLUTEN FREE TASTE OF HOME
http://glutenfreetasteofhome.blogspot.
com/2009/09/vegetarian-spring-rolls-with-thai-style.
html

I am the mother of three lovely children, one of whom has celiac disease. Celiac disease requires a 100 percent gluten-free diet, so I have learned to revise my large recipe collection to make it gluten free yet still delicious. As a freelance writer, I decided to share my tasty gluten-free recipes and news about great gluten-free products with others; this is how my Gluten Free Taste of Home blog was born.

MAKES 15

I could eat ethnic food every day and never tire of it. Spring rolls are a favorite that I order anytime they are available in Asian restaurants. Recently I learned how to make spring rolls at home! My gluten-free spring rolls taste just as good as (if not better than) many spring rolls I have tried in restaurants, and guess what? They aren't difficult to make at all, I promise. My husband and I had so much fun making them together. They were a hit with my whole family (the kiddos too), and the leftovers we had for dinner the next day tasted even better than the day they were made. My Gluten-Free Vegetarian Spring Rolls with Thai-Style Peanut Sauce are sure to become a family favorite in your household too. Both kids and grownups love dipping these fresh-tasting finger foods into the nicely seasoned peanut sauce. Whether served as a main dish, appetizer, or side dish, these beauties are delicious, satisfying, and wholesome.

THAI-STYLE PEANUT SAUCE:

½ cup warm water

1½ teaspoons sugar

½ cup creamy peanut butter (I use Earth Balance Natural Creamy Peanut Butter)

1½ tablespoons gluten-free soy sauce (tamari)

1 tablespoon coconut milk

1 tablespoon fresh lime juice

1 teaspoon Chinese chili paste (spicy or sweet, as preferred)

1 large clove garlic, finely chopped

SPRING ROLLS:

1¼ cups ounces dry rice vermicelli (thin rice noodles), or enough to yield about 1 cup cooked

1¼ cups shredded carrot

1¼ cups shredded cabbage

2 scallions, white and green parts, very thinly sliced

15 fresh basil leaves, chopped

15 fresh mint leaves, chopped

2 tablespoons chopped fresh cilantro

¼ cup peanuts, crushed

1 tablespoon grated peeled fresh ginger

1 tablespoon gluten-free soy sauce (tamari)

1½ teaspoons fresh lime juice

1 teaspoon toasted sesame oil

15 (8-inch) round gluten-free spring roll wrappers (made from tapioca or rice; found in the Asian section of your market)

1 To prepare the sauce, combine the warm water and sugar in a small bowl, stirring until the sugar is dissolved. Add the remaining ingredients, whisking until smooth and well blended. Set aside and serve at room temperature.

2 To make the rolls, bring a large pot of water to a boil over high heat. Remove from the heat and stir in the rice noodles. Let stand for 10 minutes, stirring occasionally, until soft and opaque. Drain and rinse under cold water for 30 seconds; drain again. Cut into 1-inch lengths and transfer to a large bowl.

3 To make the filling, add all the remaining spring roll ingredients except the wrappers to the noodles and mix well.

4 Prepare a bowl of warm water large enough to dip the rice papers. Working with one at a time, dip the rice paper in the warm water until it begins to soften, 8 to 10 seconds. Transfer to a flat work surface. Working quickly, put about ¼ cup filling on each wrapper. Fold the bottom of the wrapper up over the filling and then fold each side toward the center. Roll from the bottom to the top of each roll, as tightly as you can without ripping the wrapper. Wrap in plastic to keep from drying out. Repeat with the remaining wrappers and filling. Serve at room temperature, with the dipping sauce. Alternatively, refrigerate for at least 2 hours or overnight and serve chilled or return to room temperature.

Lotus Root Chips with Toasted Nori-Sesame Salt

Following the Japanese tradition of eating lotus root on New Year's Eve, I created these chips for our first New Year's celebration living in Japan. Each food eaten at New Year's Eve parties in Japan has symbolic significance. For example, long udon noodles symbolize longevity, and golden sweet potatoes express hopes for financial prosperity in the coming year. Apparently, to the Japanese, looking through the holes in the lotus root represents seeing through to the new year. It can also symbolize the wheel of life. Either way, these chips are tasty and healthy year-round as a snack or a stunning garnish. The toasted nori-sesame salt adds a unique touch to these delicious lotus root chips.

1	lotus root, 4 or 5 inches long, peeled
	Light vegetable oil for frying
¼	cup white sesame seeds, toasted and ground (or use preground sesame seeds)
¼	cup shredded nori or four 2- to 3-inch sheets, shredded
⅓	cup sea salt

RACHAEL WHITE
TOKYO, JAPAN
TOKYO TERRACE
http://www.tokyoterrace.com/2010/01/lotus-root-chips-with-toasted-nori-sesame-salt

I'm a Minnesota girl living in Tokyo, Japan. I love food (making, eating, and photographing it) and document my culinary explorations in Tokyo.

MAKES 6

1 Using a mandoline or sharp knife, carefully slice the lotus root as thinly as possible. I set my mandoline to the thinnest setting. You can go one step up from the lowest setting if that's what you prefer, but I like mine paper thin.

2 Set the lotus root slices on paper towels to remove the excess moisture. I layer mine starting with a paper towel on the bottom, then add a layer of lotus root slices, layer of paper towel, etc. Press gently on the layers to ensure the moisture is removed.

3 In a wok, heat at least 2 inches of vegetable oil. Test the oil temperature by placing a slice of lotus root in the oil. If the oil bubbles gradually, the oil is ready. If the oil immediately bubbles rapidly, the oil is too hot and the lotus root will burn. When the oil is at the proper temperature, work in batches, being careful not to crowd the lotus root. Use a slotted spoon to remove the slices as soon as they have turned brown and carefully place on a cooling rack or a plate lined with paper towels.

4 Make the toasted nori-sesame salt by placing the sesame seeds and nori in a dry pan over medium-high heat, moving the pan around to keep the seeds and nori from burning. After about 3 or 4 minutes, the nori and seeds should be fragrant and the seeds should appear slightly browned. Remove from the heat and transfer to a spice grinder or small food processor. Pulse until uniformly sized. Add the sea salt and pulse to combine the ingredients.

5 Sprinkle the lotus root chips with the salt and serve. Light, crispy deliciousness!

Lovage Spritzers

JENNY RICHARDS
SEATTLE, WASHINGTON
PURPLE HOUSE DIRT
http://www.purplehousedirt.com/content/lovage-
and-rhubarb-spritzers

Yes, we have a little purple house. And inside, outside, and all around it we try to do things with care and attention. That means growing what we can without the help of chemicals and using all the garden gives us. And what we don't grow we try to be responsible about where and from whom we buy stuff. The same rules apply in the kitchen. We try to cook as often as possible and take no shortcuts along the way. Home cooking takes time and requires skills we're likely to lose if we don't use them often. A roast chicken is the measure of a good cook. Everybody should know how to roast a chicken, and you should never stop trying to get better at it. I just don't stop at chicken.

MAKES 10

We got the idea for these spritzers after a dinner at Monsoon restaurant. One of the salads featured candied lovage—and given how much lovage we have in our garden, we were curious about how they made it. We didn't order the salad that night— too much geoduck sashimi already—but I asked the waiter if he could snatch me a little taste so I could figure out what it was. He brought back a tiny bowl of lovage stems that had been soaked in simple syrup. Our use of lovage has been limited to the leaves in things like stocks and roasted chickens—neither of us had ever thought to use the stems. We went home and made a simple syrup and soaked the stems in the syrup for about an hour (off the heat) and then added the syrup to a little sparkling water. It was cool and refreshing and a nice change from Dr. Brown's Cel-Ray soda!

¾ cup sugar

1 cup water

½ cup stems of lovage, sliced in ½- to 1-inch pieces

Lemon juice (optional)

1 Dissolve the sugar in the water in a small saucepan over medium-high heat, stirring until the liquid is clear. Add the lovage stems to the syrup and cook for 1 to 2 minutes. Remove from the heat.

2 Steep the stems in the syrup for an hour.

3 Add 2 tablespoons of the syrup, a few stems, and a spritz of lemon juice to a glass of sparkling water.

VARIATION: Use celery leaves if lovage is not available.

Mummy Juice

JANELLE
SEATTLE, WASHINGTON
TALK OF TOMATOES
http://www.talkoftomatoes.com/2007/10/26/
mummy-juice-a-batty-centerpiece

I love cooking, finding brilliant recipes, and trying new foods. This summer my family (self plus husband and two adolescent boys) cycled across Europe, then landed in Florence, Italy, for the school year. Normally from Seattle, for now I live in the heart of Tuscany. Darn, right? Recent food forays include rabbit and boar, tasting just-pressed olive oil, and learning about Italy's wine regions . . . I have been to cooking school, love to please palates, am a hawk about finding family favorite meals, and am happiest with a (wicked cool) apron on and a well-stocked fridge, freezer, and pantry.

MAKES 1 DRINK

1   cup water

⅔   cup sugar

1½ inches fresh ginger, peeled and thinly sliced

2   tablespoons fresh orange juice

1   tablespoon Triple Sec

3   tablespoons light rum

2   tablespoons club soda

When I have dinner parties, I am always excited to offer a special drink before dinner. In fact, some of my friends have come to expect it. If they show up and I am not pouring a new rosemary-infused lemon drop or marrying a bunch of rum with fancy new tropical juices or rolling up my sleeves to make the world's best Christmas Kazi, then they are sorely disappointed. So I play bartender once in a while, most notably around holidays. Admittedly the "ew, gross" look does cross my face during this drink-creating process. But it is the adjustments and imagination and "what about this?" attitude that will bring together the fun drinks that cross my table. Once the winces have subsided from awful-tasting libations, I am often left with an inventive cocktail worthy of the next dinner guest. This drink has a Halloween name: Mummy Juice. It will definitely outlast this holiday. The color, the spiciness of the ginger, the citrus notes lent by fresh oranges—this one is a keeper. To serve it, I plan on wrapping gauze around a glass before filling it to the brim. (After Halloween, we will just have to rename it Mommy's Juice—it does have a nice kick, after all.)

1 Place the water and sugar in a saucepan over medium-low heat and stir to melt the sugar. Add the ginger and let steep over low heat for 5 minutes.

2 Take off the heat and let steep until cool; strain out the ginger. (This is your ginger simple syrup.)

3 Pour 1 tablespoon ginger simple syrup, the orange juice, Triple Sec, rum, and soda into a cocktail shaker. Shake or stir.

4 Pour over ice cubes and serve (or strain and serve "up").

Martini Puffs

LINDA HOPKINS
SCOTTSDALE, ARIZONA
LES PETITES GOURMETTES
http://www.lespetitesgourmettes.com/linda/huff-and-puff

I own and operate Les Petites Gourmettes Children's Cooking School in Scottsdale, Arizona. I am mother to Marissa, twenty-two, a senior at University of Arizona; and Connor, eighteen, a freshman at Northern Arizona University. I've worked with such international chefs as Jacques Pepin, Emeril Lagasse, Yan, Ken Hom, Paula Wolfert, Nathalie Dupree, Anne Willan, and the late, great Julia Child. I've attended culinary schools in France, San Francisco, and New York. I currently am or have been involved in several culinary organizations, including Les Dames d'Escoffier International, American Institute of Wine and Food, and the International Association of Culinary Professionals. From 1999 to 2002, I was the producer of the culinary concert for the IACP Foundation, the charitable arm of IACP. Les Petites Gourmettes has been featured in *Parents* magazine, *Child* magazine, the *Arizona Republic*, the *Scottsdale Tribune*, *Cooking with Beth and Bill*, *Valley Dish*, *FamilyFun* magazine, and on all of the local Phoenix news channels for its unique focus on children's cooking. I've also had several recipes featured in cookbooks, including *Cooking with Les Dames d'Escoffier: At Home with the Women Who Shape the Way We Eat and Drink*, *Family Fun Cooking with Kids*, *Southwest the Beautiful Cookbook*, and *Reflections Under the Sun*.

MAKES ABOUT 4 DOZEN

Martinis have always seemed like such a sophisticated drink, probably in the past due to James Bond and nowadays thanks to one of my favorite television shows, Mad Men . . . Don Draper . . . deep sigh. These delectable Martini Puffs are equally upscale and easy to make, as long as you can wait the full week for the olives to marinate. Equally wonderful, they can be assembled and frozen before baking, then go directly from the freezer to the oven for impromptu entertaining.

1	10-ounce jar green olives: jalapeño, garlic, or pimiento stuffed
¾	cup dry vermouth
¼	cup high-quality gin
1	sheet frozen puff pastry
1	egg, beaten
1	tablespoon water

1 Pour olives, along with ¼ cup of their brine, into a large bowl or jar. Add the vermouth and gin, cover, and refrigerate for 1 to 2 weeks to marinate. Drain the olives, reserving the marinade for brushing the pastry and for future olive batches if desired. Place the olives on paper towels to drain further.

2 Thaw the puff pastry at room temperature for 30 minutes. Preheat the oven to 400°F. Mix the egg and water and set aside. Line a baking sheet with parchment paper or a Silpat mat.

3 Unfold the pastry sheet on a lightly floured surface. Roll into a 14-inch square. Cut into 2-inch squares. Place an olive in the center of each square. Brush the edges of the squares with the marinade. Fold the pastry up and around the olive and pinch to enclose at the top. Brush each olive package with egg wash.

4 Place the puffs 2 inches apart on the lined baking sheet. (At this point, you may freeze for 2 hours, uncovered, then re-move the individually frozen puffs from the baking sheet and quickly place in a labeled zipper freezer bag for up to 3 months. Remove as many as desired and bake directly from the freezer, adding 4 minutes to the baking time.)

5 Bake at 400°F for 5 minutes, or until golden. Allow to cool slightly, about 5 minutes. Serve warm, ideally with an ice-cold dry martini.

Okracoke Clams Casino

KIM MORGAN
CHARLESTON, SOUTH CAROLINA
A YANKEE IN A SOUTHERN KITCHEN
http://ayankeeinasouthernkitchen.com/2008/06/29/
clam-trio-clams-casino-clam-fritters-clam-chowder

Born and raised in the North, I am living in Charleston, learning to cook southern one stick of butter at a time.

SERVES 4

Clams bring back memories of summers vacationing at Ocracoke Island on the Outer Banks of North Carolina. We would rent a home on the bay and arrive armed with our trusty clam rakes, buckets, and rafts for the girls to assist us in gathering our meals. The girls would each have a designated bucket, one for steamers, one for Clams Casino steamers, and finally the bucket to hold the large chowder clams. Their dad and I would rake chest deep in water as we fought the currents. When our rakes hit a clam bed, we would call out to the girls to raft over to our spot. They would each grab clams, depending on their size, and call out "casino," "steamers," or "chowder" in excitement. Then the clams would drop into the bucket tied to the raft and they would paddle and play in the bay while waiting for the next group to be harvested. We clammed as much as two or three hours a day for our meals.

I would prepare the feast in the kitchen while they rested and napped. When they awoke they would rush to the kitchen to see what "Mom's Clam Bar" had cooking. They even made a sign that sat on the counter all week while vacationing. For our last holiday meal, once again we opened up Mom's Clam Bar and began our evening with Clams Casino. Normally you would shuck your clams for casino, but we cheated and steamed them till they just opened. They were still fantastic, and this worked out rather well.

Our next course was the Clam Fritters. The recipe made 12 to 16 more fritters than it predicted. I also was short an egg, which worked out just fine. The only thing I would change when making these again is that I would make sure that my stomach was empty—so I could eat more. We served these with a simple cocktail sauce of ketchup and horseradish along with a tartar sauce of homemade mayonnaise and chopped pickles.

The last course was clam chowder made with potatoes, celery, onions, clam broth, cream, and chopped clams. We waited an hour or so following the first two courses before enjoying a warm bowl while sitting outside watching the sun go down. It was the perfect finish to our last evening together. With lots of tears we all departed the next day, making our way to Alaska, Arizona, and Charleston. We had a wonderful trip with wonderful memories of past and new memories to share with family. I miss them all already.

24   medium littleneck (hardshell) clams

¼   cup dried bread crumbs

4   slices applewood bacon or other thick-cut bacon

2   tablespoons unsalted butter

1   cup chopped red bell pepper

½   cup chopped sweet onion

¼   cup finely chopped shallot

½   cup fresh bread crumbs

       Salt and freshly ground pepper

1 Rinse the clams until the water runs clear, free of sand. Set the clams in a sink full of cold water sprinkled with dried bread crumbs, so the clams will spit out any leftover sand, for about 30 minutes.

2 Place a rack on the bottom of a large pot. Add ½ inch of water and place the clams on the rack above the water. Cover with a lid and bring to a boil to steam the clams for about 5 minutes. Check the clams to see if they have opened or need more cooking time. When the clams open, turn off the heat. Use tongs to carefully transfer the clams and their shells to a large bowl in the sink. Discard any clams that have not opened.

3 When cool enough to handle, break the shells apart, reserving one half shell per clam and, if you like, the clam broth. Line a baking sheet with heavy-duty foil, put the clams on the half shell on the sheet, and set aside.

4 Broil the bacon in the oven until partially cooked. Cut into 1-inch pieces.

5 Pour the bacon fat into a medium sauté pan. Add the butter. Sauté the red pepper, onion, and shallot over medium heat for 5 to 7 minutes, until slightly soft. Add the fresh bread crumbs to the onion mixture and mix gently until combined. Add salt and pepper to taste.

6 Spoon 1 generous tablespoon of filling onto each clam, making sure the clams are covered well. Top each clam with a piece of bacon. Broil the clams on the second rack from the top for 2 to 3 minutes, until hot and bubbly. Serve hot.

Prosciutto-Wrapped Broccolini with Basil Crisps

1   bunch Broccolini

     Salt

1   cup balsamic vinegar

     Extra virgin olive oil

1   bunch fresh basil

     Pepper

12   thin slices prosciutto or your preferred cured meat

1 Prepare an ice bath. Trim the bottom tips off the Broccolini. Bring a large pot of water to a rolling boil. Add a generous amount of salt. Blanch the Broccolini for 30 seconds, remove, then submerge in the ice bath. When the Broccolini is fully cooled, drain and pat dry with a kitchen towel.

2 In a small saucepan, reduce the balsamic vinegar over medium heat until it becomes ¼ cup of sticky syrup. Set aside.

3 Heat about ¼ cup of olive oil in a sauté pan. Drop a small handful of basil leaves into the oil. Shield yourself from potential splatter. It takes only 1 second for the leaves to pop. Immediately fish them from the oil with a strainer and place on a towel-lined plate. The leaves should become crisp and translucent but not darkened or they will be bitter.

4 Heat a grill and coat it generously with olive oil. Grill the Broccolini until slightly charred and softened. Season with salt and pepper.

5 Wrap the Broccolini with prosciutto. Place on a serving platter and drizzle with some extra virgin olive oil and the balsamic reduction.

6 Garnish with basil crisps when ready to serve.

MELODY FURY
VANCOUVER, BRITISH COLUMBIA, CANADA
GOURMET FURY
http://www.gourmetfury.com/2009/11/prosciutto-wrapped-broccolini

I'm Vancouver's modern food culture and lifestyle ambassador. I share my culinary misadventures at GourmetFury.com and was nominated for Best Canadian Blog (10th Annual Weblog Awards), Best Food Blog, and Best Travel Blog (2010 Canadian Weblog Awards), among others.

MAKES 4

Broccolini is a cross between broccoli and gai lan, a common green used in Asian cooking. The distinct florets grow out of crispy gai-lan-like stems. Its flavor is sweeter and greener than broccoli and has a lovely tinge of bitterness. This vegetable carries its own flavour and can stand up to the saltiness of the prosciutto and the pronounced tang of the vinegar.

Neer Mor
Spiced Buttermilk

Neer mor is a refreshing summer drink made with all the goodness of buttermilk, spices, and herbs to beat the summer heat. My Amma whisked some buttermilk flavored with all fresh ingredients she had in hand and poured them into the mud/clay pots. She then served them chilled—it is true bliss to have chilled neer mor with all the fresh flavors from the herbs and the mud/clay pot. The mercury has been soaring in Seattle and its neighboring cities over the past few days, with temperatures already in the nineties. During these hot summer days I make neer mor/spiced buttermilk quite often. It is Amma's recipe to cool the body.

½   cup plain yogurt

2   cups water

1   small piece fresh ginger, peeled

1   green chile

¼   teaspoon ground cumin

    Finely chopped curry and cilantro leaves

    Pinch of asafetida (or substitute equal parts garlic and onion powder)

    Salt

1 Whisk the yogurt in a bowl until smooth. Pour in the water and churn the mixture well.

2 Smash the ginger and chile and add to the yogurt. Then add the cumin, curry leaves, cilantro leaves, asafetida, and salt to taste. Stir well.

3 Serve chilled in a glass or in a mud or clay pot.

CILANTRO
CHENNAI, INDIA
CILANTRO, COOKING WITH PATIENCE
http://cilantro-cilantro.blogspot.com/2009/06/neer-mor-spiced-buttermilk.html

I am a food enthusiast who loves to cook, try new recipes, and share the love of food through blogging. Besides cooking and blogging, I love music, travel, and gardening.

MAKES 3

Scallop Sandwiches

LEA ANN
DENVER, COLORADO
HIGHLANDS RANCH FOODIE
http://highlandsranchfoodie.wordpress.
com/2010/01/02/a-gallery-of-new-years-food

I love to cook, I read cookbooks like novels, and I love to share information with fellow foodies. Let's talk! I'm not a trained chef—I've just spent years sifting though cookbooks, recognizing the good from the bad recipes, and cooking, cooking, cooking. My theory is you just need to follow instructions well. And of course tweak the recipe to your liking. My posts include cooking adventures in my kitchen, with restaurant trips in the Denver area and beyond.

MAKES 6 SANDWICHES

These are my favorite little appetizers to make. The sweet flavors of the scallop and apricot, topped with the tangy sauce, make for an exciting flavor, not to mention an impressive display.

6   sea scallops

2   tablespoons olive oil

2   apricots

¼   cup Greek-style whole-milk yogurt

1½ teaspoons seasoned rice vinegar

     Salt and pepper

2   slices prosciutto

     Pea shoots or any sprout, for garnish

1 Pat the scallops dry and sear in 1 tablespoon olive oil in a sauté pan over medium-high heat until browned and cooked through. In the meantime, pit and thickly slice the apricots and grill in a stovetop grill pan in the remaining olive oil, until nice and hot and slightly browned.

2 In a small bowl, whisk together the yogurt, rice vinegar, and salt and pepper to taste.

3 Lay out the prosciutto on a cutting board and cut into squares that will fit nicely on top of the scallops.

4 Build your sandwiches by cutting the scallops in half to resemble a bun. Place a slice of prosciutto on the bottom half, top with a slice of apricot, and then place the top half of the scallop on top. Drizzle with the yogurt sauce, secure the sandwich with a toothpick, and garnish with pea shoots.

Tawny Manhattan

KEVIN GRAY
DALLAS, TEXAS
COCKTAIL ENTHUSIAST
http://cocktailenthusiast.com/2009/10/22/tawny-manhattan

I'm a freelance journalist and food and drink fanatic. I chronicle my exploration of spirits and cocktails at http://cocktailenthusiast.com.

MAKES 1 DRINK

The Manhattan, a classic cocktail and a favorite among serious drinkers, is a great way to pass the time. Traditionally composed of rye whiskey, sweet vermouth, and Angostura bitters, it is a perfect drink to enjoy on a cool fall day. Or any day. But with the onset of cooler weather, one might elect to change up the tried-and-true Manhattan to create a drink even more indicative of the season. With tawny port in place of sweet vermouth, the traditional Manhattan becomes a bit more complex and warms the soul as it soothes the thirsty drinker. Subbing orange bitters for angostura bitters adds a zesty citrus note to the drink, which balances nicely with the buttery, oaky flavors imparted by the port.

2   ounces rye whiskey

1   ounce tawny port

2   dashes of orange bitters

    Orange twist, for garnish

1 Stir the whiskey, port, and bitters with cracked ice until cold. Strain into a cocktail glass and garnish with the orange twist.

Seattle Food Geek's
Broiled Honey-Glazed Spiced Figs

SCOTT HEIMENDINGER
SEATTLE, WASHINGTON
SEATTLE FOOD GEEK
http://seattlefoodgeek.com/2009/09/broiled-honey-glazed-spiced-figs

Hi there, I'm Scott, and I'm a geek. It just so happens that I'm also a foodie. Being a geek and being a foodie have natural and complementary overlaps, so I guess it's not surprising to find someone who enjoys both. Like geeks, foodies are known for being dedicated to their interests. A geek might spend thousands of dollars building a computer: choosing the right motherboard, getting the fastest hard drives, water-cooling the CPU, and over-clocking the graphics card. A foodie will spend the same amount on hand-pounded copper pots, Japanese knives, artisanal olive oil, and a laser thermometer accurate to a hundredth of a degree. While geeks spend hours agonizing over every line of source code to boost performance, a foodie will pick through and carefully inspect every head of garlic in the grocery store before making a choice. We care about quality, and we're known to be a little obsessive-compulsive.

As for my foodiness, it all started in 1982, when I attended La Varenne, the prestigious French cooking school. Unfortunately, I never received a diploma from La Varenne, as I was a fetus during my tenure there. Regardless, I'm convinced that this experience had a lasting impact on my culinary development. As I grew up, both of my parents taught me the value of cooking for others. When I went off to college at Carnegie Mellon University (major geek school), I started cooking as a way to combat the stress of homework and programming assignments. Even though my college kitchen was smaller than most linen closets, I managed to produce some decent food. And once my friends found out there was an alternative to Top Ramen, filling my social calendar was never a problem. After college, I moved to Washington, D.C., to work for IBM. Unfortunately, it was a new city for me, and I didn't know many people. What was a single guy to do? Behold, the power of the dinner party: if you cook it, they will come. A few roasted hens, some wild rice, and a cheese plate were effective weapons against solitude as it turned out. You can now find me cooking nightly in my home in Seattle. I'm a very proud Microsoftee by day, but as soon as work is over, I head straight to my kitchen to cook up a storm for my girlfriend and my resident guinea pig, Rachel. Hopefully this blog will inspire you to explore your own kitchen and maybe, just maybe, discover your inner food geek.

MAKES 12 PIECES

The first signs of fall have arrived: the mornings are crisp and overcast, the slutty mannequins at the costume shop on Denny are dressed as pirates, and figs are plentiful and cheap. Fresh figs are one of the most versatile fall fruits around, and also one of the most delicious. Baked, grilled, or, in this case, broiled, they're kinda hard to screw up. For this preparation, we're glazing sliced figs with honey and spices – feel free to substitute whatever smells good to you (try Chinese five-spice powder)—then broiling until the honey caramelizes.

12   fresh figs

½   teaspoon red chili powder

½   teaspoon ground cloves

½   teaspoon ground cinnamon

¼   teaspoon ground nutmeg

¼   teaspoon paprika

3   tablespoons honey

1 Preheat your broiler and set the top rack as close to the heating element as possible.

2 Rinse the figs and pat dry. Cut off stems (optional, but the stems aren't edible). Slice the figs in half lengthwise, from stem to root.

3 Combine the dry ingredients in a small bowl (measurements are approximate—do what looks/smells/tastes good to you).

4 Lay the figs, cut side up, on a baking sheet lined with aluminum foil. Drizzle the cut side of the figs with honey. Sprinkle the spice mixture on top. Broil the figs on the top rack until the honey bubbles and just begins to brown, about 10 minutes. Watch the figs closely; cooking time will vary from oven to oven. Or you can place the figs cut side down on a hot grill for about 10 seconds. Remove from the heat and serve.

PATTY MARGUET
LOUISVILLE, KENTUCKY
EAT WITH A SPOON
http://eatwithaspoon.blogspot.com/2010/01/
vegetarian-california-rolls.html

For my day job, I'm a graphic designer. I spend nights and weekends in the kitchen, cooking. I make all of our food from scratch: bread, pasta, tortillas, sauces, etc. My husband, Jim, is my official taste tester, and we spend every night at the dining room table sharing a home-cooked meal and the high points of our day.

MAKES 8

Vegetarian California Rolls

The first time I ate sushi I popped the dollop of wasabi into my mouth and swallowed it whole . . . it took a few seconds before the vapors hit my sinuses . . . and a few seconds more before my eyes started to water. And then I heard the siren of an ambulance going by, and I remember having the hope that it was coming for me. It was the late seventies, and I was visiting a friend, Diana, in New York City. She asked me if I liked sushi and suggested we have lunch at a Japanese restaurant. Coming from a small farm in Greenville, Indiana, my experience with ethnic foods wasn't just green; it was chartreuse. I thought the strange, rectangular plate set down in front of me looked like a little stage. And I was just glad to see some rice on it . . . rice I had eaten before. After I regained my composure from the wasabi blast, I learned from my naive mistake and followed Diana's lead on how to proceed with the meal. She took me on a journey into the exotic, fresh tastes of the cuisine, and I remember being delighted with the surprises that came with each bite. Crunchy and smooth textures. Delicate and bold flavors. Cold fish and hot wasabi. It all resonated like timpani and triangles banging and pitching into my senses.

I have eaten nigiri, maki, and sashimi countless times since that blunder in the Japanese restaurant with Diana. And every time, the symphony of flavors underscores my pleasure in eating it. I actually crave it sometimes. So I taught myself to roll maki with a sushi mat — that way I can have it whenever I get the urge. Serve these vegetarian California rolls with an entree of teriyaki-marinated tuna. Or serve them with some tofu and miso soup for a vegetarian meal. But please heed this advice: make sure you dilute the wasabi!

2 cups Japanese rice

1½ tablespoons rice wine vinegar

1 tablespoon sugar

Pinch of salt

3 sheets nori

⅓ cup sesame seeds, toasted

1 medium carrot, cut into thin strips

1 small cucumber, peeled, seeded, and cut into thin strips

1 avocado, peeled, pitted, and cut into thin strips

Wasabi, soy sauce, and pickled ginger, for serving

1 Rinse the rice grains well in a fine sieve under cold water.

2 Put the rice into a medium saucepan with a tight-fitting lid. Cover it with about ¼ inch of water (2 cups). Bring the pot to a boil, give the rice a stir, and put the lid on it. Turn the heat to very low and simmer for several minutes, until all the water is absorbed.

3 Allow the rice to cool with the lid on and mix a few tablespoons of water with the rice vinegar, sugar, and salt. Fluff the rice and sprinkle on the sugar water. Fold the rice to combine it with the sugar water.

4 Cover a sushi mat with plastic wrap. Fold a piece of nori in half to break it at the seam. Lay the nori on the mat and cover it with some of the sticky rice. Sprinkle the rice with some of the toasted sesame seeds. Fold the top half of the mat over the rice and then flip the whole thing over. Now the nori is facing up.

5 Lay a few of the slices of carrot, cucumber, and avocado on the bottom edge of the nori.

6 Using both hands, roll up the bottom edge of the mat and stop at several points to squeeze it to make a tight roll.

7 Cut the roll into 8 equal pieces. Dip the top of each piece into a bowl of the toasted sesame seeds and serve with wasabi, soy sauce, and pickled ginger.

Vegetarian Scotch Eggs

SARAH
SAVOIE, FRANCE
A TASTE OF SAVOIE
http://atasteofsavoie.blogspot.com/2010/01/
vegetarian-scotch-eggs.html

I live in a small village in Savoie, in the French Alps. In a previous life I was a lawyer in Scotland, and BB was an engineer in England before we collided in the French ski resort of Courchevel in 2002. A few months later we got married, packed in our jobs, sold up everything in the UK, and headed off to France with some very basic French and a suitcase full of traveler's cheques with which we purchased our dilapidated old watermill. My Great Ambitions, when I was younger, were to write a book and own a restaurant, so I suppose writing this little blog, http://atasteofsavoie.blogspot.com, and cooking for guests in our gîte (when it's up and running) are variations on the same themes. (I had a third Great Ambition, which was to be a Backing Babe for Pink Floyd, but I don't think that's going to happen!) My blog started off as a chronicle of the renovation of the mill into a gîte, but being a keen amateur cook, it's now as much about food.

SERVES 4

Homemade Scotch eggs are nothing like shop-bought ones, which look as though they've been coated in orange sand. The egg is always overcooked, the white rubbery and grey, and the yolk anemic and dry. This version, which looks round and plump as a partridge, is a bit like all-in-one egg soldiers (one of my favourite things to eat)—a runny yolk encased in crispy fried fresh bread crumbs with the addition of some chopped fresh herbs. Delicious for breakfast or brunch.

5 medium eggs

1 dessertspoon (2½ teaspoons) finely chopped flat-leaf parsley

1 dessertspoon (2½ teaspoons) finely chopped chives

4 handfuls of fresh bread crumbs

 Salt and freshly ground black pepper

 All-purpose flour

 Vegetable oil for deep frying

1 Preheat the oven to 325°F.

2 Place 4 of the eggs in a pan and cover completely with cold water. Bring to a boil, reduce the heat, and simmer for 4 minutes. Cool in cold water before peeling.

3 Whisk the remaining egg in a shallow bowl.

4 Combine the chopped herbs with the bread crumbs in a shallow bowl and season with salt and pepper.

5 Gently roll each boiled egg in flour, then the whisked egg, and then the herbed bread crumbs.

6 Pour the oil into a pan to a depth of 2 inches and heat to 350°F. Fry the eggs until golden, turning occasionally so as not to burn, 2 to 3 minutes. Remove the eggs with a slotted spoon and place in the oven in an ovenproof dish to heat through for 3 to 4 minutes.

2 Soups and Salads

Arugula Salad with Pomegranate, Avocado, and Goat Cheese

WINNIE ABRAMSON
NEW PALTZ, NEW YORK
HEALTHY GREEN KITCHEN
http://blog.healthy-green-lifestyle.com/arugula-salad-with-pomegranate-avocado-and-goat-cheese.html

I am a naturopathic doctor turned holistic nutrition writer and recipe blogger who's kind of obsessed with all things food . . . My recipes are generally very healthy, with the occasionally decadent dish thrown in to mix things up a bit.

SERVES 2

While it may seem like a random combination of ingredients—the bitter arugula, the sweet and crunchy pomegranate, the creamy avocado, and the slightly salty goat cheese—it just works. If you don't have pomegranate molasses for the dressing, use honey instead or just leave out the sweetener. This arugula salad is lovely on its own, or feel free to add more protein for a more complete meal: cooked chicken or meat or some beans and/or nuts or seeds would all work.

SALAD:

2   large handfuls of baby arugula

     Seeds/arils from ½ a pomegranate

1   avocado, peeled, pitted, and sliced

3   tablespoons chopped cilantro or parsley

¼   cup crumbled goat cheese

DRESSING:

2   tablespoons olive oil

1½ teaspoons fresh lemon juice or balsamic vinegar

1   teaspoon pomegranate molasses

     Coarse sea salt and freshly ground black pepper

1   Toss the salad ingredients in a medium bowl.

2   In a smaller bowl, mix the olive oil, lemon juice, and pomegranate molasses. Adjust the lemon juice to taste. Pour over the salad.

3   Sprinkle with salt and pepper.

Fennel and Orange Salad with Toasted Hazelnuts and Cranberries

GIAO TRAC
MARIN, CALIFORNIA
KISS MY SPATULA | FOOD + PHOTOGRAPHY
http://kissmyspatula.com/2009/05/15/fennel-and-orange-salad/

A girl who loves being in the kitchen, behind the camera, and in front of life.

SERVES 4

1 navel orange

1 medium fennel bulb

2 teaspoons white wine vinegar

¼ teaspoon kosher salt

⅛ teaspoon freshly ground pepper

2 tablespoons extra virgin olive oil

¼ cup hazelnuts

Handful of dried cranberries

Fennel fronds, for garnish

Twizzlers were one of my favorite childhood candies. I loved twirling it around like a lasso and wearing it around my wrists like Wonder Woman's magic bracelets. So versatile. So fun. When fennel arrived on the food scene, I kept hearing how fennel tasted like licorice. Really? That weird celery-looking-thing I always pass up in the market tastes like Twizzlers?

Obviously, I had no clue. The intensely sweet anise taste and smell of fennel is so distinctive that it stands in a class all its own. The different flavor combinations and applications of fennel are truly endless: Roasted with veggies. Grilled with lamb. Baked with fish. Sautéed on its own. Stuffed with onions and pancetta. Used as stuffing. Though fennel is best in late fall and winter, I had a craving for a light and refreshing meal. This fennel and orange salad is one of my favorite salads that I happily eat year-round. It's perfect for a first course or a light meal on its own. So much better than Twizzlers. So versatile. So fun.

1 Finely grate enough zest from the orange to measure 1½ teaspoons. Cut the peel, including all white pith, from the orange with a paring knife. Then cut segments free from membranes.

2 Cut out and discard the core of the fennel bulb, then cut the bulb crosswise into very thin slices, as thin as you can get them.

3 Whisk together the vinegar, zest, salt, and pepper in a small bowl until the salt is dissolved, then slowly add the olive oil in a stream, whisking until combined well.

4 Toast the hazelnuts in a dry skillet over medium heat until fragrant.

5 Toss the fennel and oranges with the vinaigrette in a large bowl until combined well. Top with the toasted hazelnuts and dried cranberries. Garnish with a few fennel fronds.

Cedar-Smoked Asparagus Soup

DAYNA McISAAC
TORONTO, ONTARIO, CANADA
VEGAN VISITOR
http://veganvisitor.wordpress.com/2008/04/08/
cedar-smoked-asparagus-soup/

When I began blogging about food, I thought I was going to recall memories, be opinionated about where food should come from, and, hopefully, write a few decent recipes down along the way. I was not at all planning on enjoying the outcome of my photos rather than my dishes. Don't get me wrong; everything I shot I made and usually ate or fed to company shortly thereafter. Recipes still had to work well and be tasty, but I found myself stirring in the key ingredients, imagining how I might style the finished plate of food. Food is meant to look good. It's natural for it to be appealing for us to know when things are most ripe and at their tastiest, so why not photograph it from a great angle with a matching napkin?

SERVES 4

Cedar planks are not just for salmon anymore. Guests came to celebrate spring, and for that, we spark the BBQ. Having grilled on cedar planks before, I'm already fond of the fantastic smell and extra flavour it lends to food. They seem to be gaining in popularity, so finding a board isn't nearly as difficult anymore as most grocery stores with a fish department tend to carry them. The idea for the smoked asparagus soup came a little haphazardly. I was planning on grilling the asparagus with a drizzle of balsamic and olive oil, but as it was the first grill of the season the flames were uneven and the safest place not to char my freshly picked spears was up on the board. The soup came from the leftovers of the greedy three bunches that I decided to cook up for a dinner for four. The flavour was subtle and amazing. A perfect enhancement for an already pretty great vegetable.

1   cedar plank for smoking (cooking grade with no varnish)

1   medium bunch asparagus, 20 to 25 stalks

1   teaspoon balsamic vinegar

2   tablespoons olive oil

2   leeks, white and light green parts only,
    well washed and finely diced

2   cloves garlic, minced

1   medium Yukon Gold or russet potato, peeled and diced

4   cups vegetable stock

    scant ¼ teaspoon salt

1   teaspoon lemon juice (optional)

    Extra virgin olive oil, basil oil, or leek oil

1. Submerge your cedar plank in water for anywhere from 20 minutes to 4 hours, depending on the thickness of the plank and your timing.

2. Preheat a grill to medium-high heat.

3. Trim the asparagus and lay them on a large sheet of aluminum foil. Drizzle with balsamic vinegar and 1 tablespoon of the olive oil and wrap the foil to cover. Place the asparagus package on the cedar plank, lower the heat (or move the package to a cooler part of the grill), and close the lid of the barbecue. Grill for 10 to 15 minutes, checking intermittently, until tender.

4. Meanwhile, heat the remaining tablespoon of oil in a large stockpot. Add the leeks and garlic and sweat until soft and translucent but not browned, 3 to 5 minutes. Add the diced potato and cover with the stock. Bring to a simmer and cook until the potatoes are tender, about 10 to 15 minutes.

5. Remove the best spear tips from the asparagus and reserve for garnish.

6. Roughly chop the remaining smoky asparagus and add to the simmering soup. Continue cooking for another 3 to 5 minutes to merge the flavours.

7. Transfer the soup to a food processor (or use an immersion blender in the pot) and blend until smooth. Season to taste with salt and lemon juice.

8. Top each serving with the reserved asparagus tips and drizzle with extra virgin olive, basil oil, or leek oil.

Chicken and White Bean Chili

KAREN HARRIS
CASTLE ROCK, COLORADO
EAT DRINK WASH UP
http://karensrecipeforsuccess.blogspot.
com/2009/10/as-seen-in-american-in-britain.html

In 2004, I was chosen to participate in the 41st Pillsbury Bake-Off. At that contest, I won the Dinner Made Easy Category and $10,000. Since that time, I have won close to $50,000 in cash and prizes in some of this country's most prestigious amateur cooking contests. I have also had the pleasure of appearing in many television spots, including a segment on *The Martha Stewart Show* in which I prepared one of my winning recipes with her. In addition to entering cooking competitions, I write a column called "Karen's Recipe for Success" for the expatriate magazine *American in Britain*. I have a true love for cooking and eating and love rediscovering old favorite recipes and updating them for today's home cook. I also enjoy creating and sharing my own original recipes.

MAKES 9 CUPS

When my husband was first offered a job in England, we felt we needed to mull it over for a couple of days. After months of preparation, which included two garage sales and the birth of our second child, we somehow found ourselves on the outbound platform of the Gatwick Express at 6:00 a.m., in the middle of January, with two young children, six large suitcases, a stroller, two car seats, and a partridge in a pear tree. Finally, twenty hours after leaving Houston, we were in Nottingham in the little flat that my husband had called home for the few months prior to our arrival. The kitchen had everything I needed—a stove, microwave, refrigerator, and washer. The only problem was that the appliances were on a scale for Barbie and Ken's life in the UK, not ours. Oh, well, I decided to worry about that tomorrow because the newfound sensation of jet lag had set in and I felt like I had been hit by a truck. With the laundry going for the next few hours, I bundled up the children and made the trek from our flat to the Sainsbury's that was located across the street. Basically the only thing I recognized in the entire building was the produce. I have to say, I was truly amazed at the beauty and variety of the fruits and vegetables. I was mostly amazed, and still am, by the beauty that is English bacon. America could learn a thing or two from England in the bacon category.

Of course, England could learn a thing or two from America in the Tex-Mex category. Corn tortillas in a can are just unnatural in my opinion, but hey, any old port in a storm. When we needed a bit of comfort, I'd make the recipe I'm sharing with you here. It's a reflection of my roots in South Texas. Since it's on the milder side, it appeals to everyone.

4   pounds whole chicken, cut into quarters, or about 1½ pounds boneless chicken breasts and/or thighs

2   tablespoons chicken bouillon granules or chicken soup base

1   large bay leaf

1   medium yellow onion, finely diced

1   medium to large orange, red, or yellow bell pepper, finely diced

3   large cloves garlic, minced

5   tablespoons all-purpose flour

1   15.5-ounce can cannellini beans (or any other white bean), drained and rinsed

2   tablespoons mild chili powder

1   teaspoon ground coriander

2   teaspoons ground cumin

1   tablespoon chopped cilantro

1   cup single cream or heavy whipping cream

¾   cup sour cream

    Black pepper

    Chopped avocado, spring onion, cilantro, and grated cheese, for garnish

1. Rinse the chicken quarters really well and place them in a large stockpot. Add enough water to mostly cover the chicken (about 4 cups), the bouillon, bay leaf, onion, bell pepper, and garlic. Bring the liquid to a boil over medium-high heat; reduce the heat to medium, cover, and simmer until the chicken is cooked through, about 30 minutes. Remove the pot from the heat.

2. Remove the chicken quarters from the pot, transfer them to a cutting board, and cool until they can be handled comfortably. Remove the meat from the bones and chop it into small pieces; then shred slightly.

3. Remove about 1 cup of the liquid from the stockpot and set aside. Return the stockpot to medium heat and bring to a simmer.

4. Place the flour in a small bowl. While stirring constantly, gradually add the reserved liquid to the flour until a smooth paste is formed. Pour the paste into the stockpot and stir constantly until the mixture starts to thicken.

5. Add the beans, chopped chicken, chili powder, coriander, and cumin.

6. Increase the heat to medium and, stirring frequently, simmer, uncovered, for 15 to 20 minutes, or until the mixture is thick enough to coat the back of a spoon.

7. Reduce the heat to low and add the cilantro, cream, and sour cream. Stir well until the creams are completely incorporated into the chili. Add pepper to taste.

8. Serve immediately. Garnish with chopped avocado, spring onion, fresh coriander, and grated cheese.

NOTE: Like most soups, this chili is great refrigerated and served the next day, but if you intend on freezing it, leave out the whipping cream and sour cream (they separate when frozen) and add them just before serving.

VARIATION: If you'd like to spice things up a bit, add ¼ to ½ teaspoon cayenne or hot red pepper flakes for a slightly hot flavor.

Chilled Avocado and Cucumber Soup with Prawn and Scallop Salsa

DIVINA
PHILIPPINES
SENSE AND SERENDIPITY
http://sense-serendipity.blogspot.com/2009/08/
chilled-avocado-and-cucumber-soup.html

I'm a professional cook, holistic nutritionist, amateur photographer, expectant traveler, aspiring food/nutrition writer, culinary/nutrition instructor, and cookbook author. A frustrated professional dancer and violin player.

SERVES 4

This is one of the recipes I created when we had avocados growing in our backyard last August. Everyone in the family loves to eat them with milk and sugar, but I want something different. This soup is really refreshing and hydrating. The seafood garnish adds body and umami-richness to the whole dish.

CHILI-LIME OIL:

1   shallot, minced

½   teaspoon hot red pepper flakes

¼   cup grapeseed, rice bran, or extra light olive oil

    Grated zest of 2 limes

1   teaspoon water

AVOCADO SOUP:

1   large cucumber, peeled and diced

3   avocados, peeled, pitted, and diced

4   green onions, cut into 1-inch pieces

1   lime

3   tablespoons unpasteurized shiro miso (white miso)

PRAWN AND SCALLOP SALSA:

½ pound prawns, peeled

12 small or 4 large scallops, cleaned

    Unrefined sea salt

    Freshly cracked black pepper

1½ tablespoons extra light olive oil or rice bran oil

1 mandarin or Satsuma orange, peeled and segmented

8 black olives, pitted and sliced

¼ cup chopped cilantro

1. In a small saucepan, combine the minced shallot, red pepper flakes, and oil. Heat the oil over very low heat and simmer for about 3 minutes.

2. Remove from the heat and let stand for 3 minutes. Stir in the lime zest and water. Adding the water to the oil with the lime zest dissolves and carries water-soluble flavors.

3. Let stand for at least an hour, then strain the oil into a small bowl or jar. Set aside while you prepare the soup.

4. Place the cucumber, avocado, and green onions in a blender. Squeeze in the juice from the lime and add 2 tablespoons of the miso paste. Blend the ingredients, adding water to dilute the mixture until smooth and creamy. Season the soup to taste with more miso paste and lime juice if needed.

5. Transfer the soup to a large bowl, cover, and chill in the refrigerator for at least 2 hours.

6. To cook the prawns and scallops, heat a skillet over medium-high heat. Season the prawns and scallops with salt and pepper on both sides.

7. Once the pan is nice and hot, add the oil. Add the prawns and scallops and cook until they are done. Remove and transfer to a plate. Cut the prawns into 3 or 4 pieces, depending on the size, and the larger scallops in half lengthwise. Leave the smaller scallops whole.

8. In a bowl, combine the prawns, scallops, orange pieces, black olives, and cilantro. Season with a little bit of sea salt and black pepper and drizzle with a little of the the chili-lime oil to taste. Toss gently with a spoon to combine.

9. Ladle the soup into 4 individual bowls and garnish with the prawn and scallop salsa. Finish with a drizzle of the chili-lime oil.

Chilled Lettuce Soup

KATIE LERUM ZELLER
MARMANDE, LOT ET GARONNE, FRANCE
EASY GOURMET DINNERS
http://blog.easygourmetdinners.com/2009/07/
chilled-lettuce-soup-bad-market-economics.html

I'm an American expat wandering through Europe, currently living in the middle of French tomato country, restoring an old stone farmhouse with my husband. We love good wine and good food, cooking and eating. Living in France is an adventure, sometimes frustrating, sometimes funny; always interesting. It's a big world—explore it!

SERVES 2

When we lived in Andorra, a friend of mine had a long-standing, continuous argument with the greengrocer near her apartment. The produce was never fresh. The problem was clear to my friend and anyone familiar with Economics 101. She just couldn't convince the owners. It was this: the lettuce, fruits, and vegetables that were on the sidewalk for sale were old, wrinkly, gone off, wilted. In the back there was new, lovely, fresh, crisp produce. She could see it. She just couldn't get to it. The owner wouldn't move the good stuff up front for sale until the old stuff was sold. But the old stuff never sold because it was, well, old and awful. Eventually it rotted and got thrown out.

Now the stuff in back could be moved up, but by this time it was old, wrinkly, overripe, wilted. When it was moved up, new fresh produce replaced it in back, waiting its turn to wilt and be moved up front for nonsale. Obviously they sold enough of the old vegetables to keep their shop open. We assumed it was bought by the old, black-garbed widows, to make soup. We know it wasn't sold to the young, health-conscious vegetarians for salads!

Soup, like any other food, can benefit from fresh vegetables, but it has long been a dumping ground, a "just before the compost pile" place to put the last odd bits lurking in the fridge or root cellar. It's also a great place to put the less than perfect trimmings. But . . . lettuce? Why not? One puts other greens in soup . . . And when your garden starts producing too much lettuce and you start tiring of the daily salad . . . Make soup!

2   teaspoons olive oil

1   medium shallot, chopped

1   small potato, chopped

1½ cups chicken stock

4   cups shredded lettuce (such as Romaine or green leaf)

2   tablespoons snipped fresh tarragon

    Salt and pepper

4   teaspoons yogurt

1   slice bacon, fried crisp and crumbled

2   tablespoons snipped fresh basil

1 Heat the oil in a saucepan over medium heat and sauté the shallot for 2 minutes. Add the potato and stock and bring to a boil. Cover and simmer for 15 minutes. Stir in the lettuce and tarragon.

2 When the lettuce has wilted (almost immediately), remove from the heat and purée in a blender. Alternatively use an immersion blender in the pot. Season to taste with salt and pepper. Refrigerate until chilled.

3 When ready to serve, ladle into bowls, spoon 2 teaspoons of yogurt onto each serving, and sprinkle with bacon and basil.

Red Quinoa, Kale, Blood Orange, and Pomegranate Salad with Meyer Lemon Vinaigrette

I have recently fallen in love with blood oranges. I don't know whether it's the vivid red juice or the mild tart sweetness. Something about them just intrigues me. When I saw Esi's [Dishing Up Delight's] Mustard Greens and Winter Citrus Salad post, I was inspired and came up with this variation: a red quinoa salad with blood oranges, pomegranate arils, kale, and garbanzo beans tossed in a Meyer lemon vinaigrette.

It was everything I hoped it would be and more. As a bonus, this salad is absolutely bursting with health benefits. From the vitamins in the oranges, antioxidants in the pomegranate arils, protein in the quinoa and garbanzo beans, and vitamins and fiber in the kale, this salad is nearly a perfect meal. It is also bursting with flavor. The pomegranate and oranges give a fresh burst of juice and flavor, and the kale and quinoa provide a more earthy and hearty flavor. This salad is a great way to utilize winter produce and still have a fresh and bright meal.

ACTIVE FOODIE
LOS ANGELES, CALIFORNIA
ACTIVE FOODIE
http://www.activefoodie.com/red-quinoa-kale-blood-orange-and-pom-salad-with-meyer-lemon-vinaigrette/02/2010/

I'm a corporate gal with a passion for all things food and fitness. Originally motivated by an illness, I now to try to create natural and healthful dishes based on local, fresh, and organic foods.

SERVES 4

QUINOA:

2 cups water

Grated zest and juice of 1 Meyer lemon

½ teaspoon salt

1 cup red quinoa

SALAD:

1 bunch black kale

1 tablespoon olive oil

2 shallots, sliced into strips

1 tablespoon apple cider vinegar

Grated zest of 2 Meyer lemons

3 small blood oranges, peeled, pith removed, and cut into sections

1 8-ounce package pomegranate seeds

1 15-ounce can garbanzo beans

VINAIGRETTE:

Grated zest of 2 Meyer lemons

2 tablespoons honey

¼ cup extra virgin olive oil

2 tablespoons Meyer lemon juice

2 tablespoons blood orange juice

¼ cup citrus champagne vinegar or apple cider vinegar

2 tablespoons vegetable (or chicken) stock (it gives the dressing more mileage)

Salt and pepper

1 Bring the water to a boil. Add the lemon zest and juice and the salt and stir into the water. Add the quinoa and cook according to the package directions.

2 Wash the kale and let dry. Pull the leaves off the tough center stem and slice into small ribbons.

3 Meanwhile, in a large skillet, heat the olive oil and add the shallots. Sauté for about 3 minutes, until just softened. Add the kale and stir just long enough for the kale to wilt, about 1 minute. Add the vinegar and lemon zest and stir and cook for 1 minute longer. Remove the pan from the heat. Add the orange sections, pomegranate seeds, garbanzo beans, and cooked quinoa.

4 In a large bowl, whisk together the zest, honey, olive oil, lemon and orange juices, vinegar, stock, and salt and pepper to taste. Toss with the salad (there may be some extra vinaigrette).

Riley's Salmon Head Soup

LANGDON COOK
SEATTLE, WASHINGTON
FAT OF THE LAND: ADVENTURES OF A 21ST
CENTURY FORAGER
http://fat-of-the-land.blogspot.com/2009/08/salmon-head-soup.html

I'm a writer, editor, forager, and author of *Fat of the Land: Adventures of a 21st Century Forager*.

SERVES 4 TO 6

Wouldn't you know the day I forget my camera is the day my boy catches his first salmon off the beach—on a Snoopy rod no less? Riley let out a whoop when the fish hit his lure, and I'm sure I probably thought it was a false alarm, some weeds or a bottom snag. But then I saw the Snoopy rod doubled over. I ran over and set up a station behind the boy, making sure the fish didn't rip the rod right out of his grip. He reeled and kept the tip up like a pro. Pretty soon the fish was in the surf, and I figured for sure it would break the line. But Riley held on and pulled that salmon right up onto the beach.

My kids are big soup eaters. Because we live near Seattle's International District, at a tender age they discovered noodle houses and the pleasures of an Asian noodle soup. These soups are so tasty and cheap that I never really considered trying to

make my own before, but after reading Hank Shaw's post on the "nasty bits" of fish, I just had to give it a shot. Besides, we're fishermen here. When the salmon are gone, I suppose we'll fish sculpin; in the meantime we can do honor to our catch by eating every last morsel.

I haven't cooked many fish head soups. Luckily we have the Interwebs from which to draw on a nearly bottomless well of inspiration. Two recipes in particular, in addition to Hank's, informed my final improvisation: Eating Club Vancouver's Mama's Fish Head Soup is home cooking at its best and gave me the courage to use canned Szechuan prepared vegetables; a column by Steve Barnes from Albany, New York's Times Union convinced me that the double strain was the way to go and that aromatics such as green onion and cilantro would give the broth extra depth when applied after the first straining.

The advice was good. I have to say, if you'll allow me, this soup was every bit as good as soups I've had in the I-District. Those of little faith might get spooked during the proceedings, especially when the salmon heads are rolling around in there with the leeks and other stuff, going to pieces and spraying their bones about willy-nilly. But that's what the strainer is for. All the crazy stuff going into that bubbling cauldron will eventually get strained out, leaving—yes—a subtle yet profound broth in its place.

Hank's Salmon Head Soup is in the Japanese tradition. We like that—but my kids are most enthusiastic about the many varieties of Chinese noodle soup, so I went down to Uwajimaya to see what ingredients I could dig up. Sure enough, they had the sketchy can of Szechuan prepared vegetables (some sort of radish, I think). I also got some udon noodles, our nod to the Japanese style.

2 or 3 salmon heads, cut in half

3 inches fresh ginger, peeled and sliced

2 tablespoons peanut or vegetable oil

1 teaspoon toasted sesame oil (optional)

Chinese cooking wine

2 leeks, dark green tops discarded, chopped

5 cloves garlic, chopped

4 green onions, chopped

2 Thai red peppers, thinly sliced

8 cups water

1 to 2 tablespoons fish sauce (optional)

Salt

1 handful of cilantro, stemmed, with stems reserved

1 to 2 tablespoons Chinese sweet cooking wine (optional)

1 to 2 tablespoons rice vinegar (optional)

Several heaping tablespoons Szechuan pickled vegetable (optional)

1 10-ounce package Asian noodles (e.g., udon, soba, ramen), cooked or ready-to-eat

½ head napa cabbage, shredded

1 15-ounce can straw mushrooms (optional)

1 Brown the fish heads and ginger in the oils in a stockpot over medium-high heat for a few minutes, turning at least once. Deglaze the pot with a splash of wine and add the leeks, the garlic, and half the green onions and half the red peppers. Sauté together for several minutes.

2 Deglaze the pot with another splash of wine, then add the water and fish sauce. Bring to a light boil, reduce the heat, and simmer for 30 minutes.

3 Strain the contents of the pot, picking and reserving as much salmon meat as possible. Return the broth to the pot and bring back to a simmer. Taste and adjust the salt. Add half the remaining green onion and the cilantro stems. Add the Chinese sweet wine, rice vinegar, and 1 to 2 tablespoons Szechuan pickled vegetables. Simmer for another 15 to 30 minutes.

4 Strain the soup a second time and return the broth to low heat to keep it warm. Dole out the reserved salmon meat into bowls, along with noodles and a handful of shredded cabbage. Add spoonfuls of Szechuan pickled vegetables and the straw mushrooms. Ladle the broth over all. Garnish with the remaining green onion, the cilantro leaves, and the remaining Thai red pepper.

Some Like It Hot:
Roasted Poblano Vichyssoise with Lime

THE CHEF IN MY HEAD
BULVERDE/ SPRING BRANCH, TEXAS
THE CHEF IN MY HEAD
http://thechefinmyhead.blogspot.com/2009/11/
some-like-it-hotroasted-poblano.html

I love to create beautiful dishes for friends and family, aka my devoted guinea pigs. I appreciate fresh ingredients in season bursting with flavor, seafood just hours out of the water, and really good aged beef. Luckily, living in Texas, we have all of the above. Please join me on my culinary adventure, I'd love to have you along for the ride.

SERVES 10

Few people realize that vichyssoise, the cold potato leek soup with the French name, was invented not in Paris or Lyon or even in Vichy, France, but in New York City at the beginning of the twentieth century. It was 1917, and the fashionable Ritz-Carlton Hotel on Madison Avenue at 46th Street was about to open a new roof garden restaurant. The head chef was a Frenchman named Louis Diat (1885 to 1957). He often made a potato and leek soup from a recipe given him by his mother, Annette Alajoinine Diat, and he was preparing to serve it at a party celebrating the opening of the roof garden. Whether, according to legend, the soup, prepared in advance, wasn't reheated in time to be served as a first course or the day was warm and Chef de Cuisine Diat felt culinarily creative, he added cream to his mother's soup recipe and served it cold, sprinkled with chopped chives. He called it Crème Vichyssoise Glacée, or Chilled Cream Vichyssoise, in honor of the town where he was born. The original Ritz-Carlton has long since been demolished, but vichyssoise lives on. God Bless the Ritz-Carlton and all of the special memories, events, and amazing food that came from there!

Some of us love vichyssoise, as it is cool and flavorful and creamy. Some of us, such as our son, cannot wrap his head around a cold soup. To him it just doesn't make sense. Bless his heart, because in the summer he can expect to expand his taste buds with wonderful chilled soups like avocado soup, cantaloupe soup and many, many more. He'll come around. I have faith. Yesterday was one of those days I just happened to have all the right ingredients on hand, plus, I still have poblanos growing like crazy. This was my interpretation of vichyssoise.

1   pound Yukon Gold potatoes, peeled and finely diced

5   cups water

4   medium leeks, white parts only, split lengthwise and cut into ½-inch slices

1   tablespoon unsalted butter

1   medium onion, diced

2   teaspoons kosher salt

4   large poblano peppers, roasted, peeled, stemmed, seeded, and finely sliced into strips, some reserved for garnish

2   cups milk

1   cup heavy cream

1   cup half-and-half

1   cup sour cream

¼   cup fresh lime juice

½   teaspoon cayenne

    Several lime slices, for garnish

1   Place the diced potatoes in a bowl with the water.

2   In another bowl or a vegetable sink, soak the leeks in water to cover. Agitate to remove dirt and sand; drain in a colander.

3   Put the butter into a heavy soup pot over medium-low heat. Add the leeks and onion and cook until wilted. Do not caramelize, or it will discolor your finished soup. Add the potatoes with the water, the kosher salt, and the poblanos. Simmer, covered, for about 40 minutes, or until the potatoes are very soft. Add the milk, cream, and half-and-half and bring just to a boil, stirring.

4   Purée the soup in batches in a food processor or blender.

5   Return the puréed soup to a clean soup pot. Stir in the sour cream, lime juice, and cayenne. At this point you can serve the soup hot, or you can chill it for up to 1 day, covered, until it is very cold.

6   Serve the soup garnished with the remaining poblanos and slices of lime floating on top.

Spicy Pumpkin Soup

As most good things tend to end unexpectedly, mild and springlike weather in Istanbul ran away from the city all of a sudden and left a freezing cold and lots of snow in its place. A hot and tasty soup embraces various feelings like tenderness for your mom when you are sick or the nearness of a companion who makes you feel warm on a cold winter day. With these things in mind, I wanted to make a soup to enjoy while watching the snow cover everything on the street like a dusting of confectioners' sugar. No one on earth could take me out of my house for shopping so I needed to make the soup of the day with the ingredients I had on hand. I was ready to go experimental and try something like a red Mexican bean soup with fresh herbs and chili powder. Then I realized the bowl in the refrigerator full of pumpkin slices waiting for my better half to make a traditional pumpkin dessert out of them.

Pumpkin is one of those "all-purpose" foods from which you can make savory dishes, desserts, tart fillings, garnishes, and so on. Even the seed of this great-colored Halloween icon, also known as *pepita*, is a popular snack. The interesting thing is that, unlike most other snacks, pumpkin seeds are full of fatty acids beneficial to maintaining healthy blood vessels and nerves. This heart-warming and healthy soup I prepared became one of my mellow recipes for winter. Its enriched flavor with a touch of roasted mustard and coriander seeds along with grated nutmeg will make your day on a snowy winter afternoon. Taking the widespread winter laziness into account, using a large bowl to decrease the number of refill trips to the kitchen is highly recommended.

OZHAN OZTURK
ISTANBUL, TURKEY
THE KITCHEN OF OZ
http://www.thekitchenofoz.com/index.php/2010/01/spicy-pumpkin-soup/

I strongly believe that our likes or dislikes for any kind of food are just the residues of our good or bad memories rooted in our childhood and can be changed over time. A different cooking technique and a new combination of ingredients may turn the smelly cauliflower you hated from your elementary school days into a feast you would relish. Besides making people realize what they were missing until now, working in my kitchen, trying, changing, and combining various recipes provides me with relief. This is absolutely my world, with my rules, my taste, and my accomplishment at the end. My understanding of cooking is that it is a sort of performance art created by a set of pans, some kitchen utensils, and, most of all, seasonal fresh ingredients.

SERVES 6

2	cloves garlic
1	medium onion, finely diced
3	tablespoons olive oil
2	carrots, chopped
1	medium potato, peeled and chopped
3	cups chopped fresh pumpkin
4½	cups water
1	teaspoon mustard seeds
1	teaspoon coriander seeds
½	teaspoon grated nutmeg
	Freshly ground black pepper
	Sea salt
1	cup milk
	Sour cream, for garnish

1 Sauté the garlic and onion in the olive oil in a large saucepan over medium heat for 3 to 4 minutes. Add the carrots, potatoes, and pumpkin and stir to sauté. Pour in the water and bring to a boil. Tightly cover the saucepan and simmer until all the ingredients are tender, about 15 minutes.

2 Put the mustard and coriander seeds in a small saucepan over low heat, cover, and, shaking the saucepan frequently to move the seeds inside without opening the lid, cook until you hear the sound of mustard seeds popping. As you hear the last one pop, remove from the heat and crush the seeds with a mortar and pestle. Sift the spice mixture through a strainer to make sure the husks are removed.

3 Add 1½ teaspoons of the sifted spice mixture, the grated nutmeg, and pepper and salt to taste to the soup.

4 Pour in the milk and purée the soup using a hand blender or a food processor.

5 Pour the soup into bowls and serve right away. Garnish with a dollop of sour cream on top.

Thai-Style Chicken and Sweet Potato Soup

MARC AND KELLY MARINO
ACTON, MASSACHUSETTS
THE WICKED (AWESOME) WHISK
http://wickedwhisk.wordpress.com/2010/01/10/thai-syle-chicken-and-sweet-potato-soup/

SERVES 6

I came home from work one evening in a little bit of a funk. I was tired from a long day, it was cold outside, and it was one of those days where I drove both to and from work in the dark. However, all of my crankiness evaporated when I walked into the kitchen. There was a big pot of soup bubbling on the stove, and the whole house smelled like a Thai restaurant, tinged with lime and coconut.

Marc is a real soup nut. He would eat it every day if I agreed to it. On this cold night he was craving something a little different, something a little Asian and a little Caribbean. This soup was the culmination of those cravings, and as good as it smelled, it tasted even better. There was a nice meatiness from chicken and mushrooms, sweetness from sweet potato and coconut, nuttiness from peanut butter, and tang from a lime. It was a perfect balance of the different flavors and just the thing to return my mood to its normally cheerful state. So if you find yourself in need of a little cheering up, just whip up a pot of this soup, inhale the savory-sweet smell, and dig in. I guarantee you will feel better immediately.

2 tablespoons ginger oil (if you don't have any, substitute peanut or other neutral oil with minced peeled fresh ginger)

1 tablespoon minced peeled fresh ginger

1 large clove garlic, minced

1 small yellow onion, sliced

1 medium sweet potato, peeled and cut into 1-inch cubes

6 ounces white button mushrooms, stemmed and sliced

2 tablespoons fish sauce

2 cups chicken stock (homemade preferred, but if you don't have any on hand, make sure to use low-sodium broth)

2 boneless, skinless chicken breasts (about 1½ pounds), cooked and chopped

   Zest and juice of 1 lime

¼ cup chunky peanut butter

¼ cup shredded coconut, plus more for garnish

1 14-ounce can light coconut milk

   Chopped peanuts and cilantro, for garnish

1 Heat the ginger oil in a large soup pot over medium heat. Add the ginger, garlic, and onion and cook until softened, stirring often, about 5 minutes. Add the sweet potato, mushrooms, and fish sauce. Pour in the chicken stock and add water (if needed) to barely cover the vegetables. Bring to a boil, reduce the heat, and simmer, covered, for 1 hour.

2 Stir in the chopped chicken, lime zest, lime juice, peanut butter, ¼ cup shredded coconut, and coconut milk. Continue to simmer for 1 hour, stirring occasionally.

3 To toast shredded coconut for garnish, preheat the oven to 325°F and line a baking sheet with aluminum foil. Spread the coconut on the sheet and bake until browned and toasty, 8 to 10 minutes. Or toss in a dry hot frying pan until golden.

4 Serve the soup hot, garnished with toasted coconut, chopped peanuts, and cilantro.

OPTIONAL: We brined our chicken overnight prior to oven roasting. While this isn't absolutely necessary, it does add a lot of nice flavor to the chicken.

Vietnamese Tomato and Lemongrass Soup

ANDREA SPERLING
NEW YORK, NEW YORK
EATING WITH GRACE
http://eatingwithgrace.blogspot.com/2009/10/
family-day.html

I'm a foodie with a daughter who is a foodie-in-training. I believe that food is the universal language and it's what brings people together. I have a blog called www.EatingWithGrace.blogspot.com. It's about the eating adventures of a mom and daughter, with a multicultural twist. I'm also a photographer and have been eating and photographing my way around the world. I also am heading up a healthy eating initiative at a New York public school.

SERVES 4

Yesterday my screen saver's Word of the Day was "adopt." A happy coincidence since yesterday was the eleventh anniversary of when I adopted Grace from Vietnam. Most people don't tell you that when you adopt a child from another country you get the added bonus of adopting the child's culture. At first most of us who adopt internationally tend to decorate our child's room in the color of their country (lucky for me that red and yellow look nice in a kid's room), we dress them in traditional clothing on special occasions, and we learn about their culture together. As time goes on, we often learn that the easiest way to incorporate this other culture into our lives is through food. And as I have said before, Vietnam has some of the best food in the world.

Two years ago, I took Grace back to see Vietnam. One stop on the trip was Hoi An, on the south central coast. We were staying at a fancy resort that served assorted regional Vietnam dishes. The food was serviceable, but as at most hotels, it lacked any personality—or spice for that matter. Uninspired, we walked toward the local village and found a restaurant on stilts along the water that we ventured into with our friends who had accompanied us on the trip. In our family, I'm the Soup Queen as I love to make soups more than anything. Grace is the official Soup Taster.

Even though it was about 100 degrees outside, like most Vietnamese, she ordered soup. It was a tomato soup with lemongrass and Vietnamese spices. While the Soup Taster liked everything she'd eaten so far on the trip, this was the first time she said, "Mom, you've got to get the recipe." Not being able to speak Vietnamese, I knew this was going to be difficult. I tasted it, and our friends tasted it, and we all agreed that I had to figure out how to prepare it because it was worth eating again and again. When I got home, I consulted the three or four Vietnamese cookbooks I had but couldn't find the recipe anywhere. Since I could make a good Italian tomato soup, I figured it wouldn't be that difficult to adapt it and make it Vietnamese. And that seemed just about perfect since we are always happy to adopt Italian food and culture into our multicultural lives.

2 tablespoons vegetable oil

2 shallots, thinly sliced

2 cloves garlic, minced

⅛ teaspoon hot red pepper flakes

1 28-ounce can crushed tomatoes

1 pound lemongrass stalks (use only the inner yellow section so the oils are released)

1 inch fresh ginger, peeled and thinly sliced

1 tablespoon sugar

2 tablespoons nuoc nam (fish sauce)

4 cups organic chicken broth

Juice of 1 lime

Salt and pepper

Cilantro sprigs, for garnish

1 Heat the oil in a large soup pot over medium heat. Add the shallots and stir until softened. Add the garlic and red pepper flakes and stir for 1 minute. Stir in the crushed tomatoes, lemongrass stalk, ginger, sugar, and nuoc nam. Add the chicken broth. Bring to a boil, reduce the heat, and simmer for 15 minutes.

2 Stir in the lime juice and remove the lemongrass stalks. Transfer the soup to a blender in batches and purée. Or purée it directly in the pot using an immersion blender. Add the salt and pepper to taste. Add more nuoc nam and red pepper flakes if necessary. Spoon into four bowls and garnish with cilantro.

VARIATION: Add soft tofu, cut into cubes, during the last 5 minutes when the soup is simmering.

CHRISTOPHER TESTANI
BROOKLYN, NEW YORK
THE MODERN GASTRONOMER
http://themoderngastronomer.blogspot.
com/2010/01/taking-stock-ending-year-beginning-
fond_9903.html

I'm a photographer and writer with a passion for travel
and all things culinary. Born and raised in upstate New
York, I spent several years in the Los Angeles sunshine
before heading back east, where I now live in Brooklyn. Give me a bowl of homemade pasta, red wine,
some good company, and I am a happy, happy man.

White Veal Stock (Fond Blanc de Veau)

The French term for stocks, *fonds de cuisine*, literally translates as the "foundation of the kitchen." A well-made *fond de veau*, or veal stock, is anything but unimpressive or ordinary. So what exactly makes it so special? Essentially, two primary qualities: its rich yet relatively neutral flavor (which makes it versatile enough to use with nearly any dish, unlike beef or chicken broths), and the velvety mouth feel it imparts due to the high gelatin content derived from the collagen in the bones. It gives a dish that certain savory, textural quality you can't quite put your finger on, but most definitely know is in there. Basically, there's nothing else like it.

Get bones that are both meaty and have a good amount of exposed bone marrow and connective tissue. Shank, neck, back, rib, and knuckle bones are all good, and I would suggest a nice mix of a few types of these bones if it's possible. When your stock is finished, there should be enough gelatin present that the stock will solidify like a big old bowl of Jell-O in the refrigerator. If you don't have nice meaty bones, you'll probably want to add meat; otherwise you'll end up with a weak, bone-flavored stock. The ratio should ideally be somewhere around half meat, half bone.

When all was said and done, the stock turned out great and was exactly what I was looking for. Warming up my apartment on a cold winter day, filling the air with an unbelievably delicious smell (something like the best pot roast ever), and of course, filling my freezer with rich, delicious stock that I imagine will last me through the depths of winter, well into spring and beyond (if I don't get greedy). However long it lasts, I'm expecting everything at my place will taste a whole lot better this year.

MAKES 8 TO 12 CUPS

A few weeks ago, I woke up out of a much longer than usual sleep. I walked into my kitchen to begin the day and looked out the window. It was the kind of morning I imagine feels like a very late afternoon somewhere in Siberia—a cold, brooding blue refusing to acknowledge anything remotely decent or civilized. I felt it everywhere. And suddenly, inexplicably, I felt the need to make stock: a big, rich, aromatic pot of meat stock, bubbling and simmering all day long.

10 pounds meaty veal bones (shank, back, neck, knuckle)

3 cups coarsely chopped parsnips

3 cups coarsely chopped leeks, white and light green parts only

2 cups coarsely chopped yellow onions

1 cup roughly chopped celery

1 whole head garlic, halved and broken, peeled

2 ounces flat-leaf parsley

1 ounce fresh thyme

2 bay leaves

½ teaspoon whole peppercorns

Salt

1 Rinse and blanch the veal bones: Rinse the veal bones and meat with cold water and place in a 20-quart stockpot. If you have smaller pots, just split the recipe into two batches. Fill the pot with twice as much cold water as there are bones. Slowly bring to a simmer and gently move the bones around occasionally. Let simmer for about 3 minutes. Remove from the heat and quickly drain and thoroughly rinse the bones while they are still hot. Rinse and clean the stockpot.

2 Place the bones and meat back in the stockpot and add cold water until they are covered by at least 2 inches. Slowly bring to a simmer over moderate heat. Once the water comes to a simmer, skim off the fat, scum, and other particles that rise to the top. Continue to simmer and skim until this scum ceases accumulating.

3 Add the parsnips, leeks, onions, celery, and garlic to the pot. Place the parsley, thyme, bay leaves, and peppercorns in a spice pouch or tied cheesecloth, and add to the pot.

4 Gently simmer all the ingredients for 6 to 8 hours or more, until the stock tastes sufficiently flavorful and it seems that you have gotten the most out of the ingredients. Skim constantly during the simmering and add water if the liquid level falls below the ingredients. Never allow the liquid to boil, or the fats can become incorporated into the liquid, creating a cloudy stock.

5 Strain the stock through a colander or mesh strainer, then through a finer chinois or cheesecloth. Do not push down on the strainer to squeeze liquid through. The liquid should be free of any particles, with only a minimal amount of grease or fat. Repeat if necessary. Let the stock cool (preferably in an ice water bath), then place in the refrigerator until it has solidified.

6 Take the refrigerated, solidified stock and scrape any fat and grease that has hardened on the surface.

7 Reheat the stock until it has regained its liquid form and taste it for flavor and strength. If it is weak, gently simmer off some of its water content and reduce to the desired strength and concentration. Add salt to taste.

8 After the stock has cooled, it is now ready to freeze or refrigerate for later use. I freeze in 2-cup containers, along with an ice cube tray full of stock for quick, easy use.

VARIATION: To maximize the amount of stock the recipe will yield, you can also do a second extraction, or simmering of the ingredients, known as a *remouillage* (remoistening). Simply take the ingredients left over from the first straining and resimmer them in cold water, again for 6 to 8 hours, or until ready. Then repeat the straining and degreasing process and combine this second stock with the first batch. Reduce and flavor as necessary.

Wicked Good Clam Chowdah

PETER SHERWOOD
NEW YORK, NEW YORK
EVENINGS WITH PETER
http://eveningswithpeter.blogspot.com/2010/01/
clam-chowder.html

After weathering a soul-shredding career as a theatrical agent that lasted entirely too long, I left my stable of actors to pursue my literary aspirations. I am currently the dining editor for *Next* magazine (next-magazine.com/features/eats), where I write a weekly restaurant review column featuring my own food and drink recipes, culinary travelogues, and interviews with New York nightlife celebrities. I toiled as web editor for industry leader *Interior Design* magazine for several years, and I have also written for *New York* magazine, *Travel & Leisure*, and *Woman's Day*. A proud graduate of the University of New Hampshire, one of the nation's top drinking schools, I also studied voice and theater abroad at Regent's College, in London's historic Regent's Park, and at the Royal Academy of Music. I have an agent of my own now, having recently completed my first novel, and I'm in the midst of writing a second.

SERVES 4

At the ripe old age of eighty-three (he just turned so today), my dad still goes digging for clams in the summer at our cozy cottage in Friendship, Maine. He disappears for hours at a time to bring back the most delicious mollusks from Muscongus Bay, which we steam and dip in butter or marinate with gin, clam juice, and apple cider vinegar for soused clams (an excellent garnish for an extra-dry martini!) or make into a chowder. When Baby and I were home over Christmas, Dad sent us back to New York with the best gift of all—juicy clams he had dug up, vacuum-sealed, and frozen from this past summer's haul.

Although I started with a delicious recipe from my father, I feel I complicated it a bit, haphazardly trying to make my first clam chowder, but as we are to take recipes and adapt them into something of our own, passing them down along the way, I think the extra time and labor ended up creating another wonderful Down Maine dish that I'd be proud to serve in Friendship.

3   slices thick-cut bacon

2   tablespoons each chopped shallot, garlic, red onion

3   tablespoons European butter

1   cup clam liquor (take care not to put any sand
    into your chowder!) or bottled clam juice

1   can diced new potatoes, drained

1   tablespoon or so fresh thyme leaves

4 to 5 cups lobster stock

2   cups chopped clams

3   cups reduced-fat (2%) milk

    Freshly ground black pepper

    Ground white pepper

1 Cook the bacon in a skillet until crispy and remove, saving the fat. Chop the bacon when manageable. Add the fat to a stock-pot over medium heat. Add the shallot, garlic, red onion, and 1 tablespoon of butter and sauté for about 5 minutes.

2 Add the clam liquor, potatoes, and thyme with 1 to 2 cups of the lobster stock. Simmer over low heat while rapidly reducing 3 cups lobster stock over medium-high heat in a separate pan. When the 3 cups of lobster stock has reduced to 2 cups, whip the remaining 2 tablespoons of butter into it with a wire whisk and continue to simmer down to 1 cup.

3 Add the reduced stock, chopped clams, and crispy bacon to the soup and let it all get to know each other until simmering nicely. Pour in the cold milk and heat but do not boil.

4 Throw in some freshly ground black pepper and some white pepper to finish it off and let your chowder sit off the heat for at least an hour before reheating and serving. May be refrigerated for up to 2 days.

Wintery Vegetable Beef Soup

HEATHER SCHMITT-GONZÁLEZ
SOUTH BEND, INDIANA
GIRLICHEF . . . WHERE ALL ROADS LEAD TO THE KITCHEN
http://girlichef.blogspot.com/2009/12/wintery-vegetable-beef-soup-cuz-baby.html

You know how they say that music is the universal language? Well, okay, I agree with that . . . but I think that there are actually two universal languages . . . and the other is definitely food! Food unites us . . . it lets us experience one another's past, memories, emotions, and cultures. It is communal and social and inviting! And there are those of us who dream of food . . . ponder it . . . research it . . . jump in and get dirty in it! We eat with our mouths, but also with our eyes (just look at that plate!), our ears (can you hear that sizzle when the cold food hits the hot pan), our noses (um, yeah . . . scent alone can take me to another country, time, or place), and even by touch (the sense of the dough under your kneading hands or feeling the seams in the meat telling you where to cut). Food that is prepared with all of your heart and soul is the most nourishing thing in the world!

I'd love to take a culinary tour of the world . . . bit by bit, morsel by morsel . . . connecting, learning, sharing, forming new friendships . . . and I dream of an extended stay in Italy (although I'd be honored to stay anywhere in the world and immerse myself in their life for a bit).

SERVES 8

Well, it's official. It's *freeeeeezing* outside. The cold and the snow decided to take their sweet time this year . . . and then slap us in the face. Just last week it was a sorta-pleasant 48 degrees. Now it is a very unpleasant 5 (–7 with wind chill) degrees. Sure, snow's pretty . . . but ice and slick roads with black ice . . . not so pretty. I actually like being enveloped in that big white hush. As long as I can stay home all cozy and warm and see it from my window. But the minute you have to send kids out to stand at the bus and worry the whole time whether or not they'll make it home with all of their fingers and toes, it ceases being pleasant. But, imagine if you will a day where you're tucked inside the house and only know it's freezing outdoors by the icicles you can see hanging from the barren trees through your window. Nobody has to leave . . . music is playing . . . blankets are strewn from every available chair, table, and shelf to form a massive fort . . . and, of course, the kitchen is beckoning! This is when I don't mind it so much. A big pot of soup bubbling on the stove . . . that's the stuff, baby. That's the stuff.

There. Nice and cozy. Indoors with a big bowl of steaming soup. Can you see the ice on the windowpane melting from the heat in the kitchen? I can.

½   tablespoon butter

½   tablespoon oil

2   pounds beef chuck (or any tougher, stew-worthy cut)

3   quarts stock, broth, or water

4   slices thick-cut, peppered bacon

2   large sweet potatoes, peeled and diced

2   large parsnips, diced

2   large carrots, diced

2   large sticks celery, diced

1   large onion, diced

5   cloves garlic, peeled and smashed

¼   red cabbage, sliced thin

¼   green cabbage, sliced thin

A few sprigs thyme

A few sprigs parsley

2   bay leaves

Salt and freshly cracked black pepper

FOR SERVING

Balsamic vinegar

Grated Parmesan cheese

Fresh parsley, chopped

1 Begin by melting the butter with the oil in a large Dutch oven over medium heat. Add the beef and brown it well on all sides.

2 Drain off any excess fat from the pan (more than a teaspoon) and add 1 quart of stock to the pot. Bring to a boil; then reduce to simmer. Cover the pan and simmer gently until the meat is fork tender, about 2½ hours.

3 When the beef is finished cooking, transfer it to a large bowl with any juices and let cool until it can be handled; then shred it.

4 In the same pot you cooked the beef in, add the bacon and cook until just done, 5 to 7 minutes. Remove the bacon, but leave the fat in the pan.

5 Add the veggies and cook until just beginning to soften, about 15 minutes.

6 Add the shredded beef and crumble the reserved bacon back to the pot along with the herbs.

7 Add the remaining 2 quarts of stock (or more to just cover) and simmer over medium-low heat until the vegetables are tender, about 10 minutes.

8 Let the mixture sit, covered, for at least an hour to allow the flavors to come together. Then, remove the herbs and bay leaves. Season to taste with salt and freshly cracked black pepper.

9 To serve, drizzle with a glug of balsamic vinegar and grate some fresh Parmesan over the top. Sprinkle with fresh, chopped parsley and more black pepper, if desired.

ALTA
WYLIE, TEXAS
TASTY EATS AT HOME
http://tastyeatsathome.wordpress.com/2009/09/09/
vegetarian-bean-and-pumpkin-chili-plus-a-gluten-
free-cheddar-serrano-biscuit/

I cook gluten-free. I'm never afraid to try anything once (or even twice). Love to cook nourishing, healthy meals for my family—but a treat every once in a while never hurt anyone.

SERVES 8

Dear Summer: It's not that I don't love what you bring: bountiful produce, long days, and barbecue parties by the pool. It's just time to move on. As you always do around here (in Texas), you overstay your welcome, and you don't allow autumn enough time to play. So please, let's just part ways for the year. No hard feelings? I'll welcome you with open arms next June, I promise.

It's 95 degrees today here in North Texas. Hot and humid. There is a cold front in sight, they say, bringing cooler temperatures for the weekend. In my mind, it can't get here fast enough. Apparently, my appetite agrees. My husband and I have been craving cool-weather dishes. When I was planning meals this past weekend, I decided upon a vegetarian chili, cool weather or not. Even if it won't act like fall outside, I can still pretend, right? This chili will likely reappear at our home in some version several times in the coming months. It was a snap to make, with minimal prep the night before and a long, unattended simmer in the slow cooker. (Not to mention it was super-budget-friendly.)

Vegetarian Bean and Pumpkin Chili

1½ pounds mixed variety of dried beans (I used yellow-eyed peas, African red beans, and flageolets—but a mix of black, kidney, and pinto beans would work well)

1½ teaspoons ground cumin

1½ teaspoon chili powder

2 teaspoons ground coriander

½ cinnamon stick

3 teaspoons salt

Several dashes of Tabasco

2 serrano chiles, minced

3 inches chipotle chiles in adobo, minced

1 onion, chopped

3 cloves garlic, minced

1 28-ounce can crushed tomatoes

1 15-ounce can pumpkin purée

2 cups water

4 cups vegetable stock

Shredded cheese, cilantro, and sour cream, for garnish

1 Rinse the beans and soak overnight.

2 Rinse again and place the beans in a slow cooker. Add the rest of ingredients, except the garnishes, and stir well. Cook on low for 8 hours, or until the beans are tender. Taste and adjust the seasonings if necessary. Serve topped with the desired garnishes.

3 Main Dishes

Adana Kebab

I had the opportunity of spending one day (and one day only) in Turkey. I went to the beautiful city of Marmaris, which borders the Aegean Sea. Once a fishing village, Marmaris has faced incredible growth in the last twenty to twenty-five years. With a population of around 30,000, which may reach over 300,000 during high season, Marmaris nevertheless remains considerably attractive, especially due to its natural beauty. In this nice town I had a really unforgettable experience.

After the muezzin call for prayer it was lunchtime, and hence time for another meaningful experience. We wanted a rather typical place to eat, and not those regular joints full of tourists, so we went to a small diner indicated by the *narguile* salesman, a place lost in the small streets of downtown Marmaris where several of the shop owners and workers go to eat. This should mean good food at a low price (sorry, no name, no GPS markings, and no pictures of the façade, but I'm sure you'll be able to find something similar with the aid of a friendly local salesperson). The owner/chef/cook was starting to prepare "Adana Kebap." Adana is the capital of the Adana Province, while kebap (kebab) refers to dishes of plain or marinated meat either stewed or grilled. He took about 3 kg of ground mutton and worked it with a rather large knife, reducing it to almost a paste. He then cleaned 6 red bell peppers, cut them into very small pieces, and added about 6 tablespoons of cayenne pepper. These ingredients were then added to the meat, which was then worked with the knife for a few moments and then with the hands, in order to obtain a homogenous mixture. This was all; no salt was added. The mixture was then molded around wooden skewers and grilled over hot charcoal. The skewers were removed just before serving, over pita bread and along a simple but rather tasteful salad (tomatoes, onions, cucumbers, and minced mint). I've tried this recipe at home, and it worked just fine. After the meal we had a taste of *narguile* with Turkish apple tobacco. A complete success.

EUCLYDES ANTONIO DOS SANTOS FILHO
RIO GRANDE, BRAZIL
BORDERLESS COOKING
http://borderlesscooking.wordpress.com/2009/06/10/my-turkish-experience

I was born on a wonderful island in southern Brazil (Florianópolis) and presently live in the city of Rio Grande, even farther south. I hold degrees in biology and law and work as a full professor at the Federal University of Rio Grande. I have three kids: Thiago (twenty-nine), Juliana (twenty-six), and Joana (twenty).

SERVES 5

2 red bell peppers, finely chopped

2 pounds finely ground lamb

2 tablespoons cayenne

Salt

1 In a bowl, combine all the ingredients, mixing well with your hands.

2 Mold the meat around 5 wooden skewers.

3 Prepare a charcoal grill and grill the kebabs until cooked through.

4 Remove the meat from the skewers and serve over pita bread along with a simple salad of chopped tomatoes, onions, cucumbers, and minced mint.

The Philosophers' Pizza

MARIKA JOSEPHSON
MAKANDA, ILLINOIS
SHE BREWS GOOD ALE
http://shebrewsgoodale.wordpress.com/2009/12/13/
the-philosophers-pizza/

I am a cook who recently discovered the joys of home brewing. Now I'm cooking food to accompany beer (both homemade and microbrewed) in all shapes and forms.

MAKES 1 PIZZA, SERVING 2

I recently brewed my first batch of home brew, a light ale from an extract kit from Morebeer.com. It turned out unexpectedly well, and we've been enjoying it over the last couple of months straight from our very own tap. Not a tap in a Kegerator, mind you, but my jerry-rigged minifridge from the eighties that houses my keg and CO2 tank. We're finally getting to the end of the keg—I think I squeezed the last few drops out last night—but those final two pints did not go to waste; they accompanied the perfect pizza.

I lived in Italy for a year and return periodically to visit friends, eat good food, and drink good wine and beer. I learned how to make pizza from my Abruzzese friends, starting from the dough, up. Abruzzo, it is said, is the origin of Italian pizza. Philosopher #2 is part Italian and grew up in New York, eating the likes of Totonno's, Lombardi's, Di Fara, and Grimaldi's. Combined, our pizza acumen is higher than our collective IQ. I am a die-hard traditionalist when it comes to Italian food. These days I hardly ever set foot in an Italian restaurant unless I know for certain that the food is authentic (why bother?). Philosopher #2, on the other hand, grew up with an Italian-American culinary heritage, which is often ironically at odds with traditional Italian cuisine. But we both love pizza. So we combined our brains, and over the course of two years we set to work refining what would become the perfect marriage of classic Italian pizza and the best of American innovation.

We call it the Philosophers' Pizza. A traditional margherita Napoletana is extraordinarily simple. After letting the dough rise, you break a handful of San Marzano tomatoes over the top, slice a few large rounds of fresh mozzarella (*bufala*, if you prefer), drizzle olive oil on top, and sprinkle with salt. Put it in a blistering hot wood-fired oven, drop fresh basil leaves over the top, then serve. Simple. It took me a long time to break from this culinary ethic. In fact, it took the insistent threat that the pizza would simply not be eaten by my other half if we did not make a sauce, rather than utilizing straight tomatoes. Thus was born our "margherita," made with a sauce, rather than whole peeled tomatoes. It may not be exactly traditional, but it has the rest of Italy, anyway, *ed è buonissima*. Here, so you can build it from the ground up, is our recipe for the Philosophers' Pizza. Plato would have loved it, and so should you.

DOUGH (ENOUGH FOR 4 PIZZAS):

2 teaspoons active dry yeast

1⅓ cups warm water

Pinch of sugar

4 cups all-purpose flour

½ cup olive oil

1 teaspoon sea salt

TOPPING (ENOUGH FOR 1 PIZZA):

1 tablespoon chopped onion

1 clove garlic

1 tablespoon olive oil, plus more for drizzling

4 whole peeled canned San Marzano tomatoes

¼ teaspoon salt

⅛ teaspoon pepper

⅛ teaspoon dried oregano

5 ounces fresh mozzarella

5 leaves fresh basil

Parmesan cheese

1. Put the yeast in the warm water with a pinch of sugar to prime it. Let stand for 5 minutes, until small bubbles form. Add the flour, oil, and salt and mix until the dough starts to stick together.

2. On a lightly floured surface, knead the dough for 10 minutes. Put the dough in a large bowl, cover, and let sit for about an hour, or until it has doubled in size.

3. If you are making one pizza, divide the dough into 4 equal balls. Save one and wrap the other three in plastic wrap, put them in a plastic container, and put immediately into the freezer.

4. Allow the one remaining ball to rise in a bowl again until it has doubled in size, about 2 hours.

5. Preheat the oven to 425°F. If you have a pizza stone (we use one), put it in the oven now.

6. Drop the ball on a lightly floured surface and, with your fingers, lightly press down until you get a flat disk. To get a nice, even, thin crust, place your fingers at the center of the dough and press out slowly and symmetrically along an imaginary line. Rotate the dough 15 degrees and press out again. Make your hands into fists and hang the dough over them. Rotate the dough in a circle on your fists, pulling out slowly as you do so to stretch it into a wider disk.

7. Sweat the onion and garlic in a tablespoon of olive oil over medium-high heat. Break the tomatoes apart and add, with the juice, to the onion and garlic; add about 1 tablespoon more juice from the can. Let the tomatoes cook down for 5 to 7 minutes over medium heat. Add the salt, pepper, and oregano, stirring every so often.

8. If you're using a pizza peel to put the pizza on a pizza stone, cover the peel with flour to prevent the dough from sticking. Transfer the dough to the peel and add the tomatoes. Cut the mozzarella into ⅛-inch slices and place over the top of the pizza. Drizzle olive oil over the top and transfer the pizza to the pizza stone.

9. Cook for 12 to 15 minutes, until the sides become golden brown and the mozzarella begins to look like a roasted marshmallow. Cut the basil over the top right when it comes out. Grate Parmesan to taste over the top.

Asian-Braised Lamb Shanks

HEATHER WETZEL
CHICAGO, ILLINOIS
CHIK N' PASTRY
http://chiknpastry.com/2010/01/asian-braised-lamb-shanks

I'm a southern girl living in the big city. I love food and love cooking it just as much. Have been to culinary school, but work in the science/medical field, cooking on the side, rambling as I go, and telling you all the details along the way.

SERVES 4

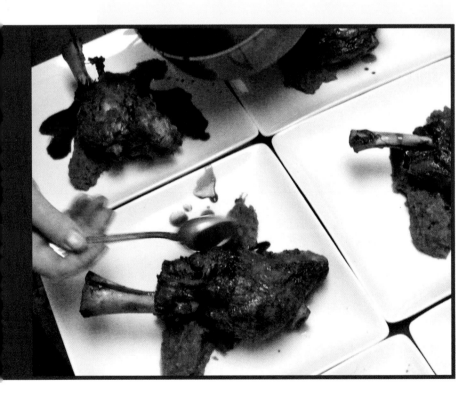

Heading to the South for the holidays involves a set to-do list: visiting Gramma; eating homemade biscuits, Aunt Faye's chicken pastry, and the rest of her spread; getting a chicken biscuit at Bojangles; finding a good North Carolina BBQ joint (complete with Cheerwine and eastern North Carolina vinegar sauce); spending loads of time with family; and going bowling with high school friends. This year, a brick oven and a guy named Mark were added to this list. Mark and his wife, Dee, are good friends with my in-laws, and they have rotating dinner parties with a decently large group of other couples. Word on the street was that Mark is a pretty hard-core cook, and so someone got this wild idea for us to hang out and cook together while Hubs and I were home for the holidays. The e-mail strings started shortly thereafter, and in no time Mark and I became cyber foodie buddies and were planning away. Food does that—it brings people together, unites them in a way that few other things can, minus sports. You cook good food, and it makes people happy. And during those few hours, we whipped up a feast for six, although it felt and looked like enough for a dozen. We threw together some pizzas with whatever was in the fridge, cooking it the "right" way via an ultra-hot wood-burning brick oven. We braised lamb shanks and served them with butternut squash (among other things) and spinach—all with an Asian flair, the night's "theme." We ate and ate and drank good wine, and then we ate dessert—a rich, creamy green tea and pomegranate panna cotta.

1   teaspoon extra virgin olive oil

    Salt and pepper

2   teaspoons five-spice powder

½   teaspoon ground cinnamon

4   whole lamb shanks

1   cinnamon stick

½   teaspoon hot red pepper flakes

1   star anise pod

3   teaspoons Chinese rice wine

⅓   cup soy sauce

2   teaspoons tamarind concentrate

2   teaspoons brown sugar

2   teaspoons chopped peeled fresh ginger

2   cloves garlic, minced

1   12-ounce bottle Chinese beer

1   tablespoon all-purpose flour (or 1 tablespoon cornstarch dissolved in a little water)

    Lime juice

1 Heat the oil in a large skillet over medium-high heat.

2 Combine some salt and pepper, 1 teaspoon of the five-spice powder, and the ground cinnamon in small bowl. Rub the spice mixture on the lamb shanks.

3 Sear the lamb shanks on each side in the hot oil until nicely browned. Transfer the shanks to a plate and set aside.

4 Preheat the oven to 225°F.

5 In a small skillet, toast the cinnamon stick, red pepper flakes, remaining 1 teaspoon of five-spice powder, and the star anise pod over low heat until fragrant.

6 In a bowl, mix the toasted spices with the rice wine, soy sauce, tamarind concentrate, brown sugar, ginger, garlic, and beer.

7 Arrange the seared lamb shanks in a large Dutch oven and pour the spice mixture over them. Cover and place in the oven to braise for 1 hour and 15 minutes.

8 Increase heat to 300°F and braise for another hour and 15 minutes.

9 Increase the heat again to 350°F and braise for 45 minutes to 1 hour, until the meat is falling off the bone.

10 Remove from the oven and keep warm.

11 Strain the braising juices into another pot. Add the flour and bring to a boil. Reduce the heat to low and simmer until the sauce is thickened. Season to taste with salt and pepper and freshen with lime juice to taste.

12 Serve the shanks with thickened sauce and your chosen sides.

NOTE: If preparing the lamb shanks ahead of time, place the shanks and thickened braising liquid back into the Dutch oven and refrigerate for up to 3 days. Reheat over medium heat, skimming any fat that has accumulated.

Authentic Bolognese Sauce

DARINA KOPCOK
VANCOUVER, BRITISH COLUMBIA, CANADA
GRATINÉE
http://gratinee.wordpress.com/2009/10/06/a-true-bolognese

I'm a food and travel writer living in Vancouver, Canada. For as long as I can remember, cooking has been one of my passions. I never aspired to be a chef. Simply, I've always wanted to be the best home cook that I can be. I began my blog, "Gratinée," as a way of documenting my adventures in the kitchen. I have learned so much through this process and have made so many wonderful friends along the way—friends who all love food as much as I do.

SERVES 8

I grew up thinking that you made Bolognese sauce by frying up some ground beef and mixing it with a bottle of Ragu. Enlightenment came in the form of a trip to Bologna itself. My first taste of an authentic Bolognese ragù took place in a trattoria close to the university in Bologna—the oldest university in the Western world. My friend Nicole ordered gnocchi and I the lasagne Bolognese. With this lasagne everything I thought I knew about Italian food slipped away. Were the noodles any better than noodles I'd had before? Was there a béchamel in between the layers of the dish? I cannot tell you. All I remember was that meat sauce, which seemed light yet deliciously rich at the same time. At the first bite a complex mélange of flavors burst across my tongue: the smokiness of good pork, the unmistakable bite of garlic and tang of onion, and other notes I could not identify. Tomato, to be sure, but not the heavy acidic tomato taste that often failed to appeal to me. Maybe it was the atmosphere that heightened the experience, but at that moment I knew that I would most likely never taste a Bolognese like that again.

Bolognese sauce is often thought to be a tomato-based meat sauce, as was my misconception for many years, but a true Bolognese actually has very little tomato. It is also served with tagliatelle noodles instead of spaghetti, or tucked in between the layers of the green lasagne Bologna is famous for. Tagliatelle are similar to fettuccine and are used because a broader noodle is a preferable cradle for a thick or heavy sauce. The ingredients in the authentic Bolognese have even been officially named by the Accademia Italiana della Cucina: beef, pancetta, onion, carrot, celery, tomato paste, red wine, and milk. This is not to say there are no variations, even in Bologna. Italians often use chopped pork or veal in their famous ragù, and chicken and goose liver may be added on special occasions. The onion, carrot, and celery can be cooked in butter as well as olive oil, and enrichments such as prosciutto, mortadella, and fresh porcini mushrooms, when they are in season, are also popular. After reading up on this classic sauce, I was ready to ditch the cream and make an authentic Bolognese. It might not be as good as the one I had in Bologna on that summer's day oh-so-long-ago, but it sure comes close.

¼ cup olive oil

4 ounces pancetta, finely chopped

1 medium onion, finely chopped

1 large carrot, finely chopped

1 celery rib, finely chopped

3 garlic cloves, minced

2 pounds ground beef

1½ cups dry white wine

1½ cups whole milk

¼ cup tomato paste

1 teaspoon salt

½ teaspoon pepper

1 In a large skillet, heat the oil over medium heat. Add the pancetta, onion, carrot, celery, and garlic. Cook until soft, 10 to 15 minutes.

2 Add the ground beef and cook until no longer pink. Stir in the white wine, milk, and tomato paste. Season to taste with the salt and pepper.

3 Simmer uncovered for 1 hour, until most of the liquid is absorbed. Serve over noodles.

KASEY FLEISHER HICKEY
SAN FRANCISCO, CALIFORNIA
EATING/SF
http://www.eating-sf.com/2009/05/different-kind-of-crepe-buckwheat.html

I'm a traveler, writer, adventurer, and food enthusiast. By day, I work in tech PR. In my free time I love to read, travel, take long walks/hikes, cook for friends, and write whenever I can. Preferably, I like to combine my traveling with my eating. I've lived in Russia, Israel, Italy, and now the United States, so my food tastes are all over the map, but I love good pasta, fresh produce, sushi, cheese, chocolate, and any Middle Eastern/Mediterranean food.

MAKES 10 CRÊPES, SERVING 2

Buckwheat Galettes with an Egg

The first time I went to Paris was with my family. I was in the ninth grade. We traveled with a tour group called Globus, and we each got a bright red bag and a seat on the double-decker bus, which promptly made stops at every landmark, but only stayed so long. I could have subsisted on *crêpes au sucre* while in Paris, if I had had my way. A savory crêpe was nowhere near my radar. To this day, I must admit that I will order a crêpe with Nutella or lemon sugar over one with ham and cheese 99.9 percent of the time. My crêpes are something of a legend among friends who have visited and been forced (forced!) to eat the breakfasts that I prepare for them. On many of these occasions, I bust out my trusty crêpe pans and whip up a batch. I then lay out a spread of jams, honey, fruit, and sugar to go along with them. When we make crêpes at my parents' house, there is often a container of caviar for those craving the savory.

I have made strides in my savory crêpe consumption—mainly fueled by my deep love of cheese and caviar. Armed with a bagful of buckwheat flour, I set out to make a different kind of crêpe: a galette (a French buckwheat crêpe). I was also ready to improve upon my experiments with eggs and try making a savory galette topped with an egg. It seemed like it would be kind of tricky at first, and I was prepared for burned fingers, but ultimately my little experiment turned out quite well—and led to some lovely pictures. I adapted a recipe by my favorite blogging Francophile, David Lebovitz. I used lower-fat milk, whole wheat flour, and halved the whole recipe. Last, I added a fun touch: an egg in the middle. One thing to keep in mind: this recipe requires some thinking ahead. You'll need to whip up the batter the night before making it. But don't worry; it'll take you only 5 minutes. The real work comes in the morning.

GALETTE BATTER:

1 cup milk (I use 2%)

1½ teaspoons sugar

Pinch of sea salt

1½ tablespoons butter, melted

¼ cup buckwheat flour

Scant ½ cup white whole wheat flour

2 small eggs

TO COOK AND SERVE THE GALETTES:

1 tablespoon milk, or as needed

Butter for cooking

2 eggs

Salt and pepper

Shaved Parmesan or Gruyère cheese (optional)

Jam or Nutella

1 Place all of the galette batter ingredients in a blender and mix until combined. Cover and refrigerate overnight.

2 In the morning, take your batter out of the fridge and let it sit for 30 to 60 minutes. Add about a tablespoon of milk and stir.

3 Place a crêpe pan over medium-high heat and melt a pat of butter in it (you can use a silicone brush to coat the pan).

4 Pour ½ cup of the batter into the pan and tilt it to swirl the batter around until it coats the pan. Your first crêpe is always going to be experimental. The fresh butter might make it a little clumpy or bubbly, and it might not cover the pan properly—don't worry; you'll get into the swing of things after one or two. Cook for about 1 minute. Use a spatula to lift an edge; if it's slightly golden and the edges are slightly crisped, it's time to flip. Once you flip, cook for another 45 seconds or so. The amount of time that you cook the galette depends on many factors: your stove, the type of pan you're using, how thick the batter is, etc. You might also need to adjust the temperature. My crêpe pans work best on medium-high heat, but this might be too high for your stove and could burn the crêpes. Start with medium heat and increase or decrease, depending on how long the crêpes are cooking.

5 I usually make 2 or 3 galettes before using my silicone brush to add a little more butter to the pan. I like to use the brush because it guarantees even coverage and never creates big clumps of butter that cause the batter to curl in places. The galettes should peel off the pan easily.

6 Here's a trick to keep the galettes warm as you cook more. Set a big pot of water on a nearby burner. Top with a large plate and bring the water to a boil. Place the finished galettes on the plate—the boiling water underneath keeps the plate warm.

7 Once you've made all of the galettes, place one back into your crêpe pan. Carefully crack one egg into the center. Use a fork to sort of spread the egg whites around the entire galette (but be careful to not disturb the yolk!). Season with salt and pepper. At this time, you could also throw in some cheese. When the whites have thickened and are universally white, use a spatula to lift the sides of the crêpe and gently fold over as you would an envelope, but leave a nice center hole for the yolk. Slide your spatula under and place on a plate. Add 4 more crêpes to each plate, to be eaten on their own or with a swipe of jam or Nutella and some berries on the side.

Carne Brasato alle Cipolle

NICOLE ALONI
SEATTLE, WASHINGTON
A CONSCIOUS FEAST
http://www.consciousfeast.com/2009/12/pot-roast-with-mushrooms-italian-style

My first two books are *Secrets from a Caterer's Kitchen* and *Cooking for Company*. My latest book, *The Backyard Bartender*, was released in May '07. In this beautifully photographed book, I have aimed to bring a chef's sensibilities and a caterer's strategies to the art of the cocktail. As befits the season, these recipes focus on the lush flavors of summer; fresh herbs and fruits are center stage. I make frequent television appearances, including on the Food Network, and most recently completed a series of interviews for KOMO News on strategic shopping. I also teach cooking and entertaining across the country at schools like Sur la Table, Draeger's, Central Market, Viking, and L'Academie de Cuisine. In addition to writing and teaching, I have served as a spokesperson for national companies and am a regular contributor to national magazines on the subjects of food, wine, and entertaining. I completed the diploma course at La Varenne in Paris, stayed on to work as a chef at châteaux in Burgundy, and owned my own vegetarian restaurant and a catering company, which also produced a line of gourmet food products. I am a member of the International Association of Culinary Professionals (IACP), Les Dames d'Escoffier, Women Chefs and Restaurateurs (WCR), Chef's Collaborative, and Slow Food. I currently live and cook in Seattle, Washington.

SERVES 6 TO 8

I created this recipe for an Italian friend who was feeling homesick. She said, "My mama used to make this wonderful roast, like an American pot roast, but with lots of garlic and herbs and wine and . . . I'm dying for some!" Picture her thick Italian accent here, I didn't have the heart to duplicate it. I whipped this up, and Marta seemed to feel it came close to her memories of home. It's so easy to make for a comforting Sunday supper. Plus, if you have a small family, the leftovers will make delicious pasta dishes, sandwiches, or noodle casseroles all week. I think it's one of the best investments of kitchen time on a blustery Sunday, like today. I'm heading for the store right now!

EASE OF PREPARATION: A snap

BEVERAGE TO ACCOMPANY: A fruity Pinot Noir

1   3- to 4-pound boneless organic beef chuck roast

    Kosher salt and freshly ground black pepper

2   tablespoons olive oil

1   pound onions, thinly sliced (about 4 cups)

3   cups sliced mushrooms (button, cremini,
    or, for a wow, chanterelles)

1½ tablespoons minced garlic

1   tablespoon tomato paste

2   teaspoons chopped fresh thyme or
    ½ teaspoon dried, crumbled

1   teaspoon chopped fresh rosemary or
    ¼ teaspoon dried, crumbled

2   cups red wine, such as Shiraz

1⅓ cups homemade beef stock or store-
    bought low-sodium beef broth

1 Place a rack in the middle of the oven and preheat the oven to 325°F.

2 Pat the beef dry and rub the roast all over with salt and pepper.

3 Heat the oil in an flameproof, ovenproof 5-quart casserole over medium-high heat until hot. Add the beef to the pan and brown well on all sides, about 6 minutes total. Transfer the beef to a plate.

4 Add the onions to the pot and sauté, stirring frequently, until soft and gold, 6 to 8 minutes.

5 Add the mushrooms, garlic, tomato paste, thyme, rosemary, ½ teaspoon salt, and ¼ teaspoon pepper and cook, stirring, for 2 minutes.

6 Add the wine and stock and bring the mixture to a boil. Return the beef to the pot, then cover tightly and braise in the oven, turning once an hour, until the beef is very tender, 2 ½ to 3 hours total.

7 Let the beef stand, uncovered, in the pan sauce for at least 15 minutes before serving.

Chapchae (Korean Stir-Fried Noodles)

This weekend is Chuseok, a national holiday in South Korea, which includes celebrations of good harvest, paying respects to ancestors, and—my favorite part—huge feasts of delicious, traditional Korean food. I'm half Korean and spent a good chunk of my childhood in Korea (my dad was in the military). One of my favorite Korean comfort foods is *chapchae* (stir-fried noodles). Not only is this dish delicious and supereasy to make, but it is also very versatile. The vermicelli noodles (made from sweet potato starch) absorb flavors very well, so any vegetable works beautifully with this recipe. You can find the Korean vermicelli noodles at most Asian specialty grocery stores—my local favorite is H Mart, which has stores in Lynnwood and Federal Way, Washington. Here is the recipe my mom and I always use. Note: For those who like their meat, feel free to add small pieces of beef or pork to this dish. Happy Chuseok, everyone!

JENN DAVIS
SEATTLE, WASHINGTON
AMATEUR GOURMAND
http://amateurgourmand.com/2009/10/02/fave-recipe-friday-happy-chuseok/

I am an "amateur gourmand" from Seattle, Washington. I am passionate about everything and anything related to the food world, so you can expect to find a wide variety of topics and information in this blog—recipes, cooking tips, local events, latest food news, restaurant reviews . . . you name it.

As a military brat, I had the unique privilege of growing up overseas and becoming immersed in different cultures and cuisines—thus my love and appreciation for food started at an early age. As a kid, while my friends were playing with Barbie dolls and stuffed animals, I was glued to my AMAZING Fisher-Price kitchen, whipping up all kinds of meals from Play-Doh. I have since upgraded to a real grown-up kitchen (albeit not much bigger than the faux one) and have learned to make meals from real, edible ingredients.

SERVES 4

8   ounces sweet potato vermicelli noodles

2   tablespoons olive oil

2   tablespoons toasted sesame oil

1   sweet onion, sliced into thin strips

2   cloves garlic, finely chopped

½   pound baby spinach, parboiled

2   carrots, julienned

3   green onions, chopped

5   mushrooms, sliced (I like to use cremini)

½   cup sliced zucchini in half-moons

3   tablespoons soy sauce

1   teaspoon sugar

    Salt

    Sesame seeds

1 Cook the noodles according to the package directions.

2 In a large pan or wok over medium heat, heat the olive oil and 1 tablespoon of the sesame oil. Add the onion and garlic and sauté for about 1 minute. Add the rest of the vegetables and cook for 4 to 5 minutes, until the vegetables are half cooked and still a bit crispy.

3 Turn the heat to low and add the cooked noodles, soy sauce, sugar, and remaining tablespoon of sesame oil. Mix to combine and cook for another 2 minutes. Add salt or more soy sauce to taste. (Or if you want it a bit sweeter, add a touch more sugar.)

4 Sprinkle sesame seeds on top before serving.

Chef Wally's Baked Papaya

CHARLES G. THOMPSON
LOS ANGELES, CALIFORNIA
100 MILES
http://1hundredmiles.blogspot.com/2009/03/chef-wallys-baked-papaya.html

I first understood the meaning of great food in 1979 while living in France and cooking for a French family. Using Julia Child's *Mastering the Art of French Cooking*, I learned to cook *à la française*. Since those early days I have worked in such restaurants as Jeremiah Tower's Stars in San Francisco, the Santa Fe Bar and Grill in Berkeley, Brendan Walsh's Arizona 206 in New York, and Restaurant Muse in Los Angeles. I was also a cheese buyer at the Oakville Grocery in San Francisco and the DDL Foodshow in New York. I have traveled and eaten my way through Europe, Mexico, South America, and the Far East. I recently decided to write about my career, experiences, and travels in the food world. I currently work as a marketing consultant for Universal Pictures, a Hollywood movie studio. I live in Los Angeles, and I am at work on my first novel.

SERVES 4

One of my earliest memories of a great dish—when I first understood that food could be amazing—took place when I was 10 years old. My mother, sister, and I lived on the Central Coast of California near Hearst Castle in San Simeon. We lived in a trailer park across Highway 1 from the Pacific Ocean, about fifteen minutes south of the castle and about twenty minutes north of Cambria. We spent many afternoons walking the rocky, usually chilly beach five minutes from home, picking up shells and rocks and collecting driftwood. After one of our afternoon walks, we returned home and upon opening the door the most wonderful, amazing smell wafted over us. I went to the kitchen and looked in the oven, and inside were six papaya halves baking away. But there was no one in the trailer. Who had made this amazing dish?

It turns out that Wally, a family friend, had come down from Carmel and, while we were out, made one of his signature dishes: Baked Papaya. For a ten-year-old it was all very magical and mysterious, and who knows how much the intervening years have affected those memories. When Chef Wally returned, we all sat down and ate the baked papayas, and they were as delicious as they smelled. I asked Wally to send the recipe, and he did.

The funny part to this story is that when I recently asked my mother about it she had to correct a few things. I thought Wally was a chef at a restaurant in Carmel. He had signed the handwritten recipe "Chef Wally." Well, as my mother patiently explained, Wally was not a chef but a traveling auto parts salesman, albeit one who liked to cook and was quite good in the kitchen. So my memory of this great chef giving me one of his coveted recipes was dashed. No matter, it's a recipe that I cherish and make to this day. This dish can be eaten alone or served with pork or fish dishes, like pork chops, roast pork, or a sturdy fish like mahimahi or red snapper. A full-bodied white wine like a Chardonnay is a good choice to accompany it.

¼   cup fine breadcrumbs

¼   cup grated Parmesan cheese

2   papayas (if green when purchased, allow to ripen 1 or 2 days until a green-yellow color and soft to the touch)

2   tablespoons butter, plus more for the topping

1   cup finely diced onion

1   tomato, peeled and chopped

Salt and pepper

1 Preheat the oven to 400°F.

2 Mix the breadcrumbs and Parmesan cheese together in a bowl and set aside.

3 Cut the papayas in half lengthwise. Remove and discard the black seeds. Dig the meat out of each half with a spoon, leaving the shell intact. Coarsely chop the papaya.

4 Heat the butter in a skillet over medium heat until it bubbles and then add the onion and cook until clear but not brown, about 10 minutes. Add the papaya meat and tomato and stir. Season with salt and pepper.

5 Continue cooking, stirring gently from time to time, until the stuffing is thick.

6 Place the papaya shells in a casserole dish in ½ inch of water so they won't burn. Spoon the stuffing evenly into the shells. Top each off with the breadcrumb–Parmesan mixture. Dot each with butter.

7 Bake for 30 minutes, or until the tops are brown.

LYNDA BALSLEV
CALIFORNIA
TASTEFOOD
http://www.tastefoodblog.com/tastefood/2009/11/
cider-braised-pork-shoulder-caramelized-onion-apple-
confit.html

SERVES 4

Cider-Braised Pork Shoulder with Caramelized Onion and Apple Confit

One of the best things about cold weather is cooking and eating comfort food. Comfort food warms us, feeding our soul and palate. It's rich, rustic, and innately appealing, reminding us of home, lit fires, baking bread, and beloved recipes we grew up eating. It also reflects the season, taking fresh, economical ingredients and slow-cooking them with rich, satisfying results.

Cider-Braised Pork Shoulder with Caramelized Onion and Apple Confit is a perfect fall dish that lands squarely in the comfort food category in my book. Pork shoulder slowly braises in apple cider and a confit of onions and apples until it is falling-apart tender. The cider and natural juices from the meat create a sweet and savory sauce. I fortify it with Calvados brandy and finish it with Dijon mustard, adding depth and sharpness to this hearty dish. As with most one-pot meals, it's meant to be eaten family-style and is easily doubled to feed a crowd. Prepare yourself: the pork will cook in the oven for several hours and fill your home with its delicious aroma. In the meantime, light a fire in the fireplace, grab that book you've been meaning to read, and curl up on the sofa with a cup of tea.

2½ pounds tied boneless pork shoulder

Salt and freshly ground black pepper

2 tablespoons olive oil

4 large yellow onions, halved and thinly sliced

¼ cup Calvados brandy

1 large Granny Smith apple, peeled,
cored, and cut into ½-inch cubes

2 cloves garlic, chopped

1 teaspoon dried thyme or 1 tablespoon fresh

1 cup apple cider

1 cup chicken stock

1 tablespoon Dijon mustard

1 Preheat the oven to 400°F.

2 Pat the pork dry and season with salt and pepper.

3 Heat the oil in a large ovenproof pot or Dutch oven with a lid. Brown the pork on all sides, turning with tongs, 6 to 8 minutes per side. Transfer the pork to a plate.

4 Pour off excess fat from the pot. Add the onions and 1 teaspoon salt. Sauté over medium heat, stirring occasionally, until the onions are very soft and deep golden brown, 18 to 20 minutes.

5 Add the Calvados and stir to deglaze the pan. Add the apple, garlic, and thyme and cook, stirring, for 30 seconds.

6 Return the pork to the pot, nestling it down in the onions. Add the cider and chicken stock. Cover the pot and place in the oven.

7 Reduce the heat to 325°F. Braise until the meat is very tender, 2½ to 3 hours.

8 Transfer the pork to a cutting board and remove the strings.

9 Boil the onion and apples until thickened and the liquid is slightly reduced, about 2 minutes. Stir in the mustard. Season to taste with salt and pepper.

10 Cut the pork into serving pieces and arrange on a platter or individual serving plates. Spoon the onion and apple confit over and around the meat.

Farm-Fresh Vegetable Stew

ALISON BERMACK
UNITED STATES
COOKING WITH FRIENDS
http://www.cookingwithfriendsclub.com/index.php?/
blog/detail/let-inspiration-strike

My fancy for cooking with a partner began in my teens, when I grew dissatisfied with my mother's dinner repertoire. I soon discovered the benefits of cooking with someone else: my father. Together we chopped, sautéed, and simmered our way through my teenage years. It became such a part of my life that my high school English teacher focused my college recommendation letter on my passion for cooking. I earned a BA in literature in English from George Washington University and an MBA in marketing from the American University. After leaving the corporate world to start a family, the challenges of delivering tasty and healthful meals grew. That's when I rediscovered the benefits of cooking with someone else. I sought compatible friends with whom to cook as a means to provide food for my family, to cater parties, and to help friends (and community members) in need. Often seen around town with sauce-splattered clothing, I started the Cooking with Friends club, an online community for sharing recipes, trading ideas, exchanging information, and scheduling cooking dates. Soon after, my best friend from childhood joined me, and we launched the Cooking with Friends website.

MAKES 3 QUARTS

I couldn't wait for my cooking date with Elisabeth. Both of our fridges were overflowing with vegetables from our farm share, five out of seven of our combined kids were back in school, and we were starved for some time to reconnect as friends. Our goals were simple: to use as many of our farm-fresh veggies as we could to create a healthy, low-fat "girlfriend" meal, after a summer filled with culinary splurges. With a bit of pressure to meet the school bus, we had only an hour and a half to cook.

The morning of our cooking date, I emptied my refrigerator, raided the pantry, and stuffed a bag with veggies, dried lentils, a few cans of beans, and a handful of herbs. When I got to her house, I quickly noticed that her counters were covered with her share of veggies—it was obvious she was just as eager. Out came the cutting boards, knives, and with no certain goal, we made whatever inspiration would strike. The garlic and onions sizzled as we chopped and diced carrots, squash, zucchini, tomatoes, peppers, and eggplant. The colorful hue of diced veggies and fragrant scent of sweet onions and garlic gave us a simple nudge; the company of a friend in the kitchen, the back-and-forth discussion of quantity, flavor, and purpose gave us the confidence to create together. Liz's kitchen was quickly filled with a sweet aroma. With a colorful pot of vegetables, kidney beans, and lentils, we arrived at a cross between a vegetable stew, ratatouille, and chili. I served it as a complement to some grilled chicken sausage for my husband for dinner, and he gave it two thumbs up.

1   eggplant

    Kosher salt

4   tomatoes

1   cup dried brown lentils

2   tablespoons extra virgin olive oil

10 cloves garlic, chopped

3   onions, diced

3   cups diced assorted peppers (sweet
    red Italian, green and red bell)

1½ cups diced carrot

½   cup chopped celery (4 ribs)

½   cup green beans, coarsely chopped

2   yellow squash, diced

1   zucchini, diced

1   teaspoon fresh thyme leaves

1   teaspoon ground cumin

1   teaspoon dried oregano

2   15-ounce cans kidney beans, drained and rinsed

1 Cut the eggplant into rounds. Lay the eggplant on a paper towel and sprinkle with kosher salt and let sit for about 15 minutes.

2 Remove the skins from the tomato, either with a soft-skin peeler or by scoring the tops, blanching the tomatoes in boiling water, and then slipping off the skins.

3 Cook the lentils in boiling water for 8 minutes, drain, and run under cool water.

4 In a large stockpot, heat the olive oil over medium heat. Sauté the garlic for just a minute and add the onions. Season with 2 teaspoons kosher salt and cook for about 10 minutes.

5 Begin adding the other vegetables gradually, starting with the peppers, carrot, celery, and green beans. Add the eggplant after its salting period and add the squashes last.

6 When all the vegetables are in the stew, add the thyme, cumin, oregano, and 1 tablespoon plus 1 teaspoon salt. Let the vegetables simmer until tender as a stock begins to form. Mix in the lentils and kidney beans. Simmer on low for as long as you have, up to an hour and a half.

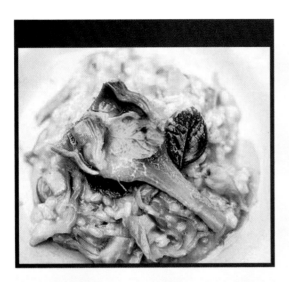

ASHLEY AND JASON BARTNER
PIOBBICO, PESARO URBINO, ITALY
LA TAVOLA MARCHE
http://latavolamarche.blogspot.com/2010/02/
heavenly-artichoke-risotto.html

We are all about local seasonal Italian recipes, organic gardening, food festivals and markets, and day trips in Le Marche, Tuscany, Umbria, and beyond. *Tutti a tavola!* (All to the table!) We are American expats living the dream in the Italian countryside and own an *agriturismo* (organic farm inn) and cooking school. From the hustle-bustle of life in Manhattan to organic farmers and innkeepers, our life took a 180. We celebrate life at every meal, from the farm to the table. What better way to know a culture but through its food? Jason is a professional chef and cooking instructor with years of experience as an executive chef in New York. Ashley is a host-extraordinaire and writer for *Italia!* magazine.

SERVES 6

Heavenly Artichoke Risotto

Overflowing crates of artichokes fill the market streets in central Italy, a sure sign that spring is on its way. So what to do with these edible flowers? Try one of my faves, artichoke risotto. We love to serve this for Easter feasts as well. (If artichokes seem a bit overwhelming and you wonder where to begin, look no further than our post on cleaning artichokes at http://latavolamarche.blogspot.com/2009/05/art-of-choke-how-to-clean-artichoke.html.) This recipe takes about an hour total time, and yes—you've gotta stir the risotto constantly. It's a labor of love, and your work won't go unnoticed; hence the clean bowls. You'll find some recipes with shortcuts; however, to really get the creamy chewy consistency, you must work the starch from the rice, and that means good old-fashioned elbow grease.

8   fresh artichokes

Juice of 1 lemon

Extra virgin olive oil

1   onion, chopped

1   clove garlic

5   cups or so fresh vegetable stock

2   scant cups risotto rice—Arborio or Carnaroli is best

¾   cup dry white wine

Salt and pepper

Grated Parmesan cheese

1 Start by cleaning your artichokes and soaking them in lemon water (made by adding the lemon juice to 8 cups of water).

2 Heat ¼ cup olive oil in a pan, add the onion and garlic, and cook for 10 minutes or so over medium-low heat without browning.

3 Chop up your artichokes, add them to the pan, and sauté them slowly until tender—so you could mush with a fork.

4 Add a couple of spoonfuls of vegetable stock to help the process along and keep from browning the 'chokes.

5 Now raise the heat, add the rice, and sauté for a minute or two. Add the wine and let it cook out a bit.

6 Season with salt and pepper.

7 Meanwhile, bring the remaining stock to a boil in another pan.

8 Add a ladleful of the hot stock and cook, stirring, until it has been absorbed into the rice.

9 Continue adding the stock, a ladleful at a time, stirring constantly until each addition has been absorbed. This will take 18 to 20 minutes.

10 When the rice is al dente, turn off the heat, add the grated cheese, and give the rice one more stir. Check the seasoning. The rice should be thick and creamy but not runny. Cover the pot and allow the rice to sit for a couple of minutes.

11 To serve, spoon the rice into bowls and sprinkle with more Parmesan, drizzle with extra virgin olive oil, and serve immediately.

VARIATION: Buy a couple of extra 'chokes and top the dish with the hearts, steamed or boiled separately.

Homemade Tagliatelle with Wild Boar Ragù

LAUREL LYMAN
LOS ANGELES, CALIFORNIA
CORKPOPPER
http://blog.cork-popper.com/2009/11/16/week-11-what-to-eat-with-the-2006-badia-di-morrono-teneto/

I'm a twenty-something professional with an absolute obsession for all things food and wine. I am usually planning dinner before I've had lunch, and my favorite time of the week is Sunday evening, when my boyfriend and I cook that week's CorkPopper dinner together.

SERVES 6

One of my favorite Italian dishes comes from Tuscany, Tagliatelle with Wild Boar Ragù. Tagliatelle is a wide, long pasta that looks much like a thick ribbon, while ragù is a traditional Italian meat sauce. Wild boar (*cinghiale* in Italian) is a Tuscan staple. This rich, savory dish may just be the ultimate in comfort food and will pair perfectly with the big, complex flavors in a Badia di Morrono Taneto wine.

As you can imagine, wild boar can be difficult to find, so it's probably easiest to order it online. I got mine from Broken Arrow Ranch (http://www.brokenarrowranch.com), a specialty site that sells only wild boar, antelope, venison, and elk meat. Be sure to start the sauce several hours before dinner so that it has time to simmer. If you don't want to make your own pasta dough, the fresh pasta you can buy at the grocery store is fine, although you're unlikely to find tagliatelle (fettuccine will probably be the widest you can get).

RAGÙ:

1¾ pounds wild boar loin

    Freshly ground pepper and salt

    All-purpose flour

    Extra virgin olive oil

1   large brown onion, chopped

6   cloves garlic, minced

1   large carrot, finely chopped

1   celery rib, finely chopped

¼   pound pancetta, cubed

1   28-ounce can crushed tomatoes

½   bottle dry red wine

⅓   cup chopped flat-leaf parsley

8   fresh basil leaves, chopped

TAGLIATELLE:

1   cup unbleached all-purpose flour plus more for dusting

1   large egg, beaten lightly

½   tablespoon extra virgin olive oil

1½ tablespoons cold water

    Freshly grated Parmigiano-Reggiano cheese, for serving

1   Season the boar with salt and pepper and dust with a bit of flour.

2   Brown the boar on both sides in a large skillet over medium heat.

3   Heat a couple of tablespoons of olive oil in a pot until almost smoking. Add the onion and cook until translucent. Add the garlic and cook for a couple minutes longer before adding the carrot and celery. Cook until the vegetables are soft.

4   Add the boar and pancetta to the pot and cook for 10 to 15 minutes.

5   Add the tomatoes, wine, parsley, and basil. Simmer for several hours, stirring occasionally.

6   After a couple of hours, pull apart the boar meat. You should be able to do this just with a wooden spoon.

7   To make the tagliatelle, blend the flour, egg, oil, and water in a food processor until the dough just begins to form a ball, adding more water drop by drop if the dough is too dry. The dough should be firm and not sticky.

8   Pulse the dough for 15 seconds more to knead it.

9   You can prepare the dough up to 4 hours ahead of time. Just keep it covered in the fridge. It needs to stand, covered, at room temperature for an hour before you roll it out, however, so keep that in mind.

10 To roll pasta dough, set the smooth rollers of a pasta machine at the widest setting. If you don't have a pasta roller, use a rolling pin; it'll just take some elbow grease and you may not be able to get it very thin.

11 Divide the dough into 3 pieces. Flatten one piece into a rough rectangle and cover the remaining pieces with an inverted bowl. Dust the rectangle with flour and feed it through the rollers. Turn the dial down one notch and feed the dough through the rollers.

12 Continue to feed the dough through the rollers, turning the dial one notch lower each time, until the dough has reached the desired thinness. The dough should be a smooth, long sheet 4 or 5 inches wide and about $\frac{1}{16}$ inch thick.

13 Roll the remaining pasta dough in the same manner.

14 Using a knife, cut the sheets of pasta into 1-inch-wide ribbons.

15 Once you have all your tagliatelle cut, cook in a large pot of boiling salted water. Fresh pasta takes only a couple of minutes to cook, and it's done when it floats to the top, so be sure you've already set the table and are ready to eat.

16 Drain the cooked pasta (don't rinse!) and divide among large pasta bowls. Cover the pasta with sauce and sprinkle with grated Parmigiano-Reggiano cheese. Serve with crusty grilled bread and a simple side salad.

How Sweet It Is Sweet Potato Lasagne

SHELLY HUANG
NEW YORK, NEW YORK
EXPERIMENTAL CULINARY PURSUITS
http://experimentalculinarypursuits.wordpress.
com/2009/11/03/how-sweet-it-is-sweet-potato-
lasagne

Experimental Culinary Pursuits is all about discoveries in culinary therapy and everyday delights. I believe that the creation of food should be an inventive art, leaving the chef free to dream up possibilities to fulfill his or her taste buds' desires. So I devote time in the kitchen to experimentation, conjuring up new marriages of ingredients and flavors. I have a strong olfactory sense and take pride in distinguishing perfume notes in blind tests, which allows me to imagine how a dish would turn out by smelling the raw ingredients. Food is the essence of life and forever connected to our stories and experiences, so here is also where I write about my stories and how they connect to these food creations. The recipes you'll find here are almost always vegetarian, but I think of this blog as much more flexible, and I hope the stories inspire you to try your own twists to make these dishes your own. Thanks for joining me on my adventure.

Outside of the kitchen, I work as a brand marketer in the business of "making women pretty" and love to spend weekends exploring New York City and contemplating life in Central Park.

SERVES 6

When I was a child, I loved to listen to my grandmother tell me magical stories of historic Taiwan. As she cooked my favorite breakfast meal—sweet potato congee—she would recall the days during the Japanese occupation, when food was scarce and they had to survive on a diet of sweet potatoes and rice. Though times were tough, the picture she conjured was full of warmth: families roasting these orange wonders by the bonfire while children ran around chasing fireflies. While the sweet potato congee simmered, she would make the little side dishes to complete that heavenly breakfast: sautéed spinach with black mushrooms, Asian eggplant with basil, and egg omelet with soy sauce, brown sugar, and pickled radish.

With the craziness of work and life, I haven't been able to see my grandparents in almost two years, and I miss them dearly. So I made this sweet potato dish in a moment of nostalgia, taking inspiration from all the yummy Taiwanese dishes that nourished my little tummy, but putting on a Westernized spin by layering it into a sweet potato lasagne and infusing it with culturally diverse flavors. I marinated the eggplant in a blend of olive oil and Italian herbs, tossed the spinach and portobello mushrooms with heavy cream and cheeses, and dipped the sweet potatoes in dry curry powder. You may think with the mish-mosh of herbs and flavors that it's a totally crazy dish. But trust me—it worked! The result was a burst of complementary flavors that tasted as familiar as my grandma's love, but with an exotic twist that ventured into a new territory. I just wish I could cook this for her someday soon.

4 sweet potatoes

3 tablespoons curry powder

2 cups olive oil

1 large eggplant, sliced

3 tablespoons dried basil

   Salt and pepper

10 ounces fresh spinach, chopped

12 to 15 baby portobello mushrooms, sliced

1 to 2 tablespoons vegetable or canola oil

2 jalapeño chiles, chopped

½ cup half-and-half or heavy cream

12 ounces grated Monterey Jack and
    cheddar cheese mix, divided

2 cups marinara sauce

1 Preheat the oven to anywhere between 350° and 375°F (whatever is most convenient if you're baking something else at the same time).

2 Slice the sweet potatoes ½ inch thick and marinate in dry curry powder mixed with 1 cup of olive oil. Set aside.

3 Slice the eggplant crosswise 1 inch thick and marinate with the remaining 1 cup of olive oil, the basil, and some salt and pepper. Set aside.

4 Sauté the spinach and mushrooms in the vegetable oil until cooked. Add the jalapeños for some spice.

5 Turn the heat down and add the heavy cream and half of the cheeses to make a creamy, not watery, mixture.

6 Layer the ingredients in a 9 by 12-inch pan in this order: half of the sweet potatoes, half of the spinach/mushroom mixture, half of the eggplant, all of the marinara sauce, and then the remaining half of the sweet potatoes, spinach and mushroom mixture, and eggplant. Finally, sprinkle the remaining cheese blend on top.

7 Bake for 30 to 45 minutes, until heated through.

8 Devour with passion.

Jade Buddha Salmon Tartare

DAVID ROLLINS
MONTREAL, QUEBEC, CANADA
THE DOG'S BREAKFAST
http://the-dogs-breakfast.com/?p=393

SERVES 2 AS A MAIN COURSE,
4 AS AN APPETIZER

This simple and elegant treatment for salmon was inspired by a spectacular spicy beef tartare we tasted at Marché 27, just down the street from where we live. The dish featured two favourite flavours—the smoky burn of chipotle and sweet sting of red chile. We re-created it at home a week later in what we call "the Saturday night test kitchen" and were inspired by this success to create a spicy Thai beef tartare. The first attempt was a surprising disappointment. We make a brilliant yellow Thai curry paste that braises incredibly well with pork loin and coconut milk. I could taste in my mind how perfectly this curry would work in a tartare, with its structured layers of flavour: an earthy base of roasted cumin and turmeric; the bright heat of ginger, garlic, and bird's eye chiles; and a sparkling top note of lemongrass and cilantro stems. A squeeze of lime, and we'd be in tartare nirvana. Not so. We underestimated the importance of cooking the paste, and the raw curry had little flavour. While trying to enjoy it, we planned the second attempt. Frying the curry would release and bind the flavours; some raw onion would add needed bite. And perhaps raw beef was not the best platform for these flavours anyway?

So we set out a second time, with salmon. And let's not use the curry we saved; let's start with green onion. And some chives and cilantro leaves. And a little lime zest. And a squeeze of juice. Hmm. It's all green. Do we have any green chiles? No, but a bit of wasabi might do. No, try the green habanero sauce and grate some ginger. More lime? Something brighter. Champagne vinegar. Yes. Pepper. Salt. Done. And in 10 minutes we had created what we now think (after trying it again several times) is the first original masterpiece to emerge from "the test kitchen." The only improvement we made the second time around was to add Thai basil, green chiles, and a more aromatic pepper, some wild Madagascar pepper we picked up at Olive et Epices in the Jean-Talon market over the weekend. Grinding it in the mortar and pestle released an intensely fragrant aroma, resinous and woody, like hot cedar tears. Don't overdo the lime juice or the salt. And be sure to add the lime juice and vinegar at the last minute, to avoid cooking the tartare. Serve with mashed avocado and thin slices of day-old baguette, brushed with oil and baked until golden.

12	ounces raw salmon, finely diced
2	tablespoons chopped green onion
1	tablespoon chopped chives
1	tablespoon chopped cilantro
1	tablespoon chopped Thai basil
2	teaspoons grated peeled fresh ginger
	Grated zest of 1 lime
	Habanero sauce and minced green chile
	Salt and pepper
	Olive oil to coat
	Good squeeze of lime juice
1	teaspoon champagne or rice vinegar

1 Combine all the ingredients except the lime juice and vinegar.

2 Chill for 30 minutes.

3 Add the lime juice and vinegar, adjust to perfect, and serve.

Layered Tuna Sashimi Salad

BRAD WHITE
TOKYO, JAPAN
TOKYO TERRACE
http://tokyoterrace.com/2009/09/16/returning-the-favor-hubby-guest-blog

I love life, my beautiful wife, Rachael, awesome family and friends, teaching elementary kids, making music, travel, photography, mountains, and enjoying my wife's amazing food creations.

SERVES 4

Watching *Julie and Julia* with Rachael this summer, I felt as though I was watching hidden camera footage from the last year or so of our life since Rachael started her food blog. My incredible wife, the brains and heart behind Tokyo Terrace, is constantly whipping up new recipes and ideas for her site. Seeing "Julie" and her hubby go through the joys and struggles of this food blog world was an interesting look in the mirror. Nearly every day, I get to come home to a meal for which I would gladly pay top dollar in a restaurant anywhere in the world. The photos and recipes she posts just can't do it all justice. As of this week, it has been five years since our first date (back in college, when Rachael cooked for us using only a dorm microwave).

Thinking about all this reminded me that Rachael deserves the same kind of treat that I get to enjoy so often. Today I tried, in my I-don't-really-do-this-since-I'm-married-to-a-fantastic-cook kind of way, to return the favor. After school finished and my second graders went home, I went to one of our favorite local indoor markets for some "inspiration," as Rachael calls it. Once I passed by a beautiful piece of fresh tuna, I knew I had to buy it. After wandering aimlessly for a few minutes, I saw some avocados in another store and had an idea. How about some sort of inside-out tuna roll . . . minus the rice? Next were a little Boston-Bibb-type lettuce, some red cabbage, and a couple green onions for extra color, texture, and flavor. My idea was to have alternating layers of green and red, and to my surprise, it worked!

So, here is my first and only Tokyo Terrace recipe: "Bradley-san's layered tuna sashimi salad." There's no rice in this recipe, but I suppose that could also make a nice base or side dish next time around. Cheers to Rachael for all the wonderful things she does here at Tokyo Terrace. Happy anniversary, hon—I hope you enjoyed your night off!

⅓ cup light soy sauce

1½ tablespoons wasabi paste

⅓ cup thinly sliced green onions

1 head Boston or Bibb lettuce

½ head red cabbage

2 ripe avocados

1 pound sashimi-grade tuna (we used Chu-toro)

1 In a small bowl, whisk together the soy sauce and wasabi paste.

2 Place all but 2 tablespoons of the sliced green onions in the sauce bowl and set aside, allowing the wasabi and green onions to infuse the soy sauce as you prepare the rest of the salad.

3 Rinse the lettuce and red cabbage. Finely shred the red cabbage.

4 To assemble the salad, start by placing leaves of lettuce around the bottom of a salad bowl. This is the foundation of the salad.

5 Once there is a full layer of green lettuce, create a layer of the red cabbage on top. As much as possible, form a pyramid of lettuce by concentrating the slices in the middle of the bowl. Set the bowl aside as you prepare the avocado and tuna.

6 Cut the avocados in half lengthwise. Remove the pit. One easy way to do this is to hold one half of the avocado in one hand and strike the pit with the sharp part of a chef's knife. Twist slightly and the pit comes out smoothly. Then slice the avocado lengthwise into ¼-inch-thick slices. Remove the slices from the skin with a spoon, taking care to keep the long slices intact.

7 Continue building your pyramid by overlapping the slices of avocado with one end of each slice always in the center of the bowl (like bicycle spokes from a center hub).

8 Now slice the tuna into ½-inch slices. Make an X by putting your sharp knife perpendicular to the natural lines of the tuna. Slice at about a 45 degree angle, pulling the knife toward you as you cut.

9 Repeat the same procedure as with the avocado, creating an overlapping layer of tuna on top of the avocado slices. Drizzle the salad with the soy-wasabi dressing and sprinkle with the reserved 2 tablespoons green onions.

Luscious Thai Chicken Pineapple Curry

NANCY
EUROPE
SPICIE FOODIE
http://spiciefoodie.blogspot.com/2009/09/luscious-thai-chicken-pineapple-curry.html

Spicie Foodie is a blog penned by me, Nancy, a 30-year-old Mexican expatriate living in Europe. The idea of starting my very own foodie blog came as a needed distraction and because I wanted a place to catalog all of my recipes and kitchen experiments. As a child I avoided the kitchen and my mother's constant (failed) attempts to get me to learn to cook. Over the past few years I finally gave in and have been teaching myself how to cook, as well as trying to learn to bake. I have lived outside of my native country for most of my life, but the dishes of Mexican cuisine are ones that will be part of me and my menus as long as I live. My favorite foods or those I crave the most are spicy flavorful dishes; I guess it's only natural being that it's in my blood. I like to cook a large range of spicy dishes from Mexican, Indian, and Thai cuisines, as well as less spicy dishes from a range of other countries

SERVES 4

Thai cuisine is one that has been greatly influenced by its surrounding neighbors. To me, the most obvious influence has been from Indian cuisine on the curries. Thai food is unique in that it has created this perfectly balanced harmony of five flavors that are present in every dish or in every meal. The flavors are salty, sweet, sour, bitter/aromatic, and hot/spicy, not particular to that order. Some samples of how the flavors are brought into a dish can be salty from shrimp paste or fish sauce, sweet from sugar or sweet fruits, sour from lemon or lime juice, bitter/aromatic from bitter melons or aromatic herbs and green vegetables, hot of course from chiles or curry paste. Though not included in the five main flavors, but common in many dishes, is the sweet creaminess of coconut milk. When most people think Thai food, they think hot! But it's not all about the chile; it's about bringing out those flavors that complement each other. I love spicy food, but spicy to where it doesn't overpower the rest of the dish. What's the point then? Might as well grab whole chiles and start munching away (ouch—better grab the antacids). When I've heard people say they have never tried or don't like Thai or other "spicy" cuisines because they are not able to handle the spiciness, it makes me feel a bit sad. To me it's a pity for people to miss out on such scrumptious meals when they really shouldn't have to. (By the way, my recipes can all be adjusted to fit your personal "heat" level.)

Today I have a big favorite of not only mine but my husband's and that of one of our frequent dinner guests, Thai chicken pineapple curry with cherry tomatoes and bamboo shoots. Just writing this makes my mouth water. It's so easy and fast to make, I guarantee they'll want seconds. The curry paste I used is my own from the previous recipe found here, http://spiciefoodie.blogspot.com/2009/09/red-thai-curry-paste-krung-kaeng-phed. Covering the essentials of Thai cuisine, we have a deliciously fruity, spicy and sweet, creamy curry, with aromas that will have them all running to the dinner table. This dish makes great leftovers—that is, if you have any left.

2   boneless, skinless chicken breasts

1   tablespoon oil

1   tablespoon grated peeled fresh ginger

2   cloves garlic, minced

2   tablespoons red curry paste

½   cup chicken broth or ½ bouillon cube

1   teaspoon sugar (omit if using canned pineapple)

½   teaspoon ground turmeric

½   cup sliced bamboo shoots

1   cup chopped fresh pineapple in bite-sized pieces

1½ tablespoons fish sauce

1   fresh red chile, sliced, extra spicy (optional)

1   cup coconut milk

12 red cherry tomatoes

    Fresh basil leaves or cilantro, for garnish

1 Dice the chicken into thick bite-sized pieces. In a large pan or wok, warm up the oil, then add the chicken and cook all the way through. Next add the ginger and garlic, cook for a few minutes, and add the curry paste. Stir to combine with the chicken. Add the chicken broth, sugar, turmeric, bamboo shoots, pineapple, and fish sauce. Stir in the red chile. Cover and simmer over medium heat for about 10 minutes. Add the coconut milk and stir, then add the cherry tomatoes and cook for another 5 to 8 minutes, until the tomatoes are soft.

2 Done! Or you can let it cook a bit longer until you are ready to serve. When serving, add a couple of fresh basil or cilantro leaves for garnish. Serve with steamed white rice.

VARIATION: You can use drained canned pineapple if fresh isn't available, but it tastes so much better with fresh.

Meatloaf with an Asian Twist

When I was growing up, Christmas meant my father would be making his special stuffed chicken. He would always remind my mom, "Mi, just make sure it's the JUMBO chicken," as she was the one in charge of going to market to buy the bird. Stuffed chicken is his specialty since he makes it himself. You see, it's rare to see the men of my family in the kitchen, as servants would always do the cooking in the Philippines.

Papa would make two stuffed chickens: one for our family, one for the archbishop. When I was married, he would make three: an additional one was given to my in-laws. And then when my sister was married, he started making four . . . you get the picture. Now, every holiday season, my father makes six. The process of preparing his stuffed chicken involves the entire household, whether it's with deboning the chicken, or buying the ingredients, or decorating and plating and styling the chicken. It was a family effort that said, "Our family made this especially for you!" The final touch to this Christmas tradition was that the chickens were personally hand-delivered.

SKIP TO MALOU
SAN DIEGO, CALIFORNIA
SKIP TO MALOU
http://www.impromptudiva.com/2009/12/lessons-my-papa-taught-me.html

I'm a wife and a mom to three wonderful kids. I cook simple dishes and put my take on traditional ones. I draw my inspiration in creating dishes from my family and friends. Skip to Malou is all about home-cooked meals, and there is no better way to enjoy good food than to share with you the dishes I prepare and the stories that come with it.

SERVES 6

As for me, my butchering skills are not good enough yet for me to completely debone a chicken. Nonetheless, I'm still going to honor my papa's tradition. I am going to do a spin on traditional meatloaf, by using the same ingredients as my papa would use for his stuffed chicken to cook an Asian-inspired meatloaf. I invite you and your family to take part in our family's tradition. While baking it, the aroma from the kitchen flows out into the living room, and you will hear your family ask, "Mom, what are you cooking? It smells so good." You know it's the aroma from the bacon blending with the flavors of the meatloaf. Slowly, they will all come to the kitchen table, and pretty soon you will be hearing, "Is it dinner yet, Mom?"

3   dinner rolls (you could use bread slices)

⅓   cup milk

5   tablespoons hoisin sauce

5   tablespoons oyster sauce

1   cup ketchup

5   large eggs, 3 of them hard-boiled

1   large onion, chopped

4   cloves garlic, minced

1   teaspoon salt (word of caution: go slow on the salt; it will make or break the recipe)

    Pepper

4   pounds ground beef

10   strips bacon

1 Preheat the oven to 400°F.

2 Break the bread into small pieces, put into a small bowl, and stir in the milk. Set aside.

3 Meanwhile, in a large bowl, mix the hoisin sauce, oyster sauce, ¾ cup of the ketchup, and the 2 raw eggs. Add the onion, garlic, salt, and some pepper.

4 Add the bread-milk mixture and mix until well combined. Add the ground beef and mix gently.

5 Oil a baking sheet using cooking spray or line the pan with foil. Place the meat mixture on the prepared baking sheet and form into a loaf. I use a baking pan to shape it. Make sure to press it hard to make it compact. When baked it will give you a solid meatloaf.

6 Dig a canal down the center of the loaf. Add the peeled boiled eggs to the canal. Mold the meat mixture over the eggs to cover completely.

7 Baste the meatloaf with the remaining ¼ cup ketchup. Arrange the strips of bacon on top.

8 Bake until the meat is cooked, 45 to 55 minutes. Let it rest for 10 minutes before slicing and serving.

Melt-in-the-Mouth Paneer Kofta

SANJANA MODHA
NOTTINGHAM, ENGLAND
KO RASOI
http://korasoi.blogspot.com/2010/01/how-long-did-you-think-it-would-be-i.html

I'm Sanjana, a 21-year-old food-obsessed British-born Indian. I hope you like Indian food, because there are rickshaws full of it at KO Rasoi. So come and take a peek inside my little vegetarian kitchen, where I will share my most beloved family recipes, inspired creations, passion for ingredients, and all things food.

SERVES 6

I can't resist the rich, creamy, irresistible goodness of a good paneer with kofta. Kofta (as they are usually referred to in the South Asian subcontinent) have a heavy presence over various cuisines, from the Arabian peninsula to what was once Persia to North Africa and Eastern Europe. The concept of the kofta (or kufteh, köfte, keftes, kufta, ufta, etc.) is that ground ingredients are spiced (according to which herbs and spices are predominantly available in that country) and rolled into a certain shape—usually spherical, but in some Arab counties they are shaped rather like long kebabs. Kofta can be fried, steamed, grilled, or baked.

I liken this particular recipe to a softer version of the Italian potato dumplings, gnocchi, whereas nonvegetarian kofta would most likely equate to meatballs in Italy. Ground meat is usually the key ingredient, but here at KO Rasoi I like to do things a little differently, so, being the "paneer monster" that I am, I gave in to my yearnings. This recipe makes the softest, melt-in-the-mouth kofta coated with the silkiest, delicate spicy-sweet sauce you have ever tasted. If this hasn't sold you, then the combination of honey, fennel, and cardamom in the tomato, almond, and cashew nut sauce will get your taste buds dancing to a Bollywood beat!

KOFTA DOUGH:

2 cups paneer (fresh or grated on the fine side of a cheese grater if you are using a block of paneer)

⅓ cup mashed potatoes, passed through a sieve

1 tablespoon minced peeled fresh ginger, lightly sautéed

2 cloves garlic, minced and lightly sautéed

1 green chile, minced and lightly sautéed

2 tablespoons finely chopped fresh coriander

1 teaspoon baking powder

1 teaspoon lemon juice

Salt

SAUCE:

¾ cup skinless almonds, blanched until tender

¾ cup cashews, blanched until tender

1 cup water

¾ cup minced onion

1½ tablespoons ghee (clarified butter, available at Indian markets)

½ teaspoon cumin seeds

¼ teaspoon asafetida (or equal parts garlic and onion powder)

2 tablespoons minced peeled fresh ginger

1 tablespoon minced garlic

1 tablespoon minced fresh red chile

¼ cup plus 2 tablespoons tomato paste

1 teaspoon ground cumin

1 teaspoon ground coriander

2 teaspoons ground fennel

2 teaspoons clear honey

1 teaspoon ground cardamom

Salt

Chopped fresh coriander (optional)

TO COOK THE KOFTA:

Oil for deep frying

3 tablespoons cornstarch

1 Mix all the ingredients for the kofta in a bowl and bind them together like dough. Set aside.

2 For the sauce, grind together in a food processor or blender the almonds, cashews, water, and onion. Set aside.

3 Heat the ghee in a large nonstick pan over medium heat and add the cumin seeds, asafetida, ginger, garlic, and chile. Sauté for a couple of minutes, then add the tomato paste and ground almond and cashew paste. Cook until oil emerges on the surface.

4 Add the cumin, coriander, fennel, honey, and cardamom powder. Cook for a further 3 to 4 minutes and adjust the thickness of the sauce with 2 to 3 cups water. Season with salt and garnish the sauce with a little chopped coriander if you wish.

5 Roll the kofta into small palm-sized oval shapes, making sure there aren't any cracks in them. Use a little oil to prevent the dough from sticking to your hands.

6 Heat enough oil in a pan to deep-fry the kofta. Roll the kofta in a little cornstarch and dust any excess away. When the oil reaches 350°F, add the kofta and fry over medium heat until they are a very light golden colour. Drain on paper towels.

7 Assemble the dish just before serving by gently mixing the kofta with the sauce. You can make this ahead of time by keeping the kofta and sauce separate until you are ready to serve.

Mentaiko Kimchi Udon

MOMOFUKUFOR2
VANCOUVER, BRITISH COLUMBIA, CANADA
MOMOFUKU FOR 2
http://momofukufor2.com/2010/01/mentaiko-kimchi-udon-recipe

Whenever I travel, noodle restaurants are on my list of places to visit. In 2007, I visited New York, and one of the places I wanted to eat at most was Momofuku Noodle Bar, but it almost didn't happen without a lucky string of delayed flights, fluky taxi drop-offs, and the willingness to wait 45 minutes for the restaurant to open. A couple of years later I had my wedding and honeymoon in New York City. Instead of taking care of wedding details, I hit up all four Momofukus (there happen to be five 'fukus now, but it's a good excuse to go back). It was absolutely delicious: a fried chicken feast, the Ko lunch menu, watching the chicken wing chef lovingly caress each wing before plating—these are memories that last a lifetime, my friends. This year, I got the *Momofuku Cookbook* for Christmas. I sat myself on the couch and read the entire book cover to cover on Christmas Day. It was the best cookbook I ever read. After I finished, I realized two things: (1) it would be superyummy to cook every recipe in this book, and (2) why not put up a site where I could write and take photos of the process?

SERVES 4

What do you do when you have excessive amounts of homemade kimchi in the fridge? Make *mentaiko* kimchi udon, of course. I first had this dish at Zakkushi, a Japanese charcoal grill restaurant. One bite of those springy, chewy wheat-flour noodles tossed with spicy roe and kimchi and I was hooked. I can eat plates and plates of this stuff. So with an abundance of happy fermented kimchi in the fridge, I decided to do just that: eat plates and plates of the stuff.

I love all kinds of noodles, but udon holds a special place in my heart. I've always enjoyed thicker noodles, mostly for the chewy bite they have. There's a world of difference within the varieties of packaged udon you buy at the supermarket, so I say, find the kind you like and stick with it. For me, that brand is frozen Maruchan Kame Age Udon. I find frozen udon superior to the udon you buy refrigerated or vacuum packed. The noodles taste fresher, are more slick and chewy, and have a slight rectangular quality. They taste great just in a plain broth or even better as *mentaiko* kimchi udon. *Mentaiko* is known as Japanese spicy cod roe, but really it's pollock roe. It's marinated in salt and red pepper and has a rich, creamy flavour with a reddish hue. Originally *mentaiko* was Korean, which explains why it pairs so well with kimchi. *Mentaiko* kimchi udon is so ridiculously easy to make that I wish I had *mentaiko* all the time. You can purchase it at most Japanese grocery stores or maybe even Korean ones.

2   tablespoons butter

1   sac of mentaiko

2   bricks frozen udon

2   tablespoons kimchi

Sliced green onions and nori (dried seaweed sheets), for garnish

1 Melt the butter over low heat. Set aside to cool to room temperature.

2 Remove the roe from the sac. Cut the sac open with a knife and use a spoon to scrape the eggs out.

3 Bring a pot of water big enough for your 2 bricks of udon to a boil over high heat. Cook the udon according to the package directions.

4 Mix the mentaiko and butter together.

5 Drain your udon, and while it is hot, toss it with the mentaiko butter. Once the udon is coated, add the kimchi and toss well.

6 Sprinkle with sliced green onions and nori.

Nasi Minyak (Malaysian Festive Rice)

The Malay community traditionally prepares *nasi minyak* during festive occasions, like Eid Mubarak or weddings.

2   tablespoons ghee (clarified butter, which you can find easily at any Indian grocery store)

1   large onion

2   cloves garlic

1   teaspoon grated peeled fresh ginger

1   stick cinnamon

3   star anise

3   cloves

3   cardamom pods

5½ cups water

½   cup evaporated milk

1   cup basmati rice, washed, soaked, and drained

½   teaspoon salt

GARNISH:

1   tablespoon fried onions

1   tablespoon raisins

1   tablespoon slivered cashews

    Green onion and cilantro, thinly sliced

ZAIANNE SPARROW
SCHAUMBURG, ILLINOIS
ZAIANNE SPARROW
http://www.zaianne.com/2009/11/19/beef-rendang-nasi-minyak-malaysian-festive-rice

SERVES 6

1   Heat the ghee in a pan over medium heat and fry the onion, garlic, ginger, cinnamon, star anise, cloves, and cardamom pods until fragrant.

2   Put the water, evaporated milk, and rice in a rice cooker pot. Add the spiced onions to the pot of rice and stir, mixing the ingredients well. Add the salt and close the lid.

3   When the rice has cooked, sprinkle the garnishes on top and serve.

RENA WASSER AND TOM SPERBER
TEL AVIV, ISRAEL
THE ROYAL KITCHEN
http://theroyalkitchen.blogspot.com/2010/02/steak-with-onion-and-tomato-sauce.html

We met in a party bathroom and since then have been roaming around, searching only for the best things in life. We are spoiled and critical, but our snobbery comes from the heart. If you find something good, drop us a line.

SERVES 2

2   tablespoons olive oil

3   cloves garlic

2   tablespoons chopped fresh ginger

½   tablespoon black peppercorns

1   large onion, diced

1   tomato, peeled, deseeded, and roughly chopped

½   cup white or red wine

2   tablespoons balsamic vinegar

1½ cups water

1   tablespoon salt

3   tablespoons sugar

1   teaspoon black pepper

1   teaspoon ground coriander seeds

½   teaspoon dried red chili

2   6 to 8-ounce New York strip steaks

Steak with Onion and Tomato Sauce

We had a long day working at home and we craved something a bit decadent for dinner. It was a matter of minutes before we realized we had two beef fillets waiting in the freezer! With no extra thought, we defrosted the steaks and threw together an incredible onion and tomato sauce to go with them. The result was just perfect.

1 To make the sauce, heat 1 tablespoon of olive oil in a medium pot over medium heat. Slice 2 cloves of the garlic. Sauté the garlic, ginger, peppercorns, and onion for 10 minutes or until golden brown.

2 Mix in the tomato and let simmer for 2 minutes.

3 Add the rest of the ingredients—first the liquids, then the spices—and mix well. Bring to a boil and let simmer on low heat, stirring occasionally, for 25 minutes or until only thick fluid remains.

4 For the steaks, rub them on both sides with the remaining 1 tablespoon of olive oil. Chop the remaining clove of garlic and rub it into both sides of the steaks as well. Then, sear them in a very hot skillet on all sides.

5 Let them cook for 10 minutes more on each side over medium heat.

6 When the steaks are cooked to your preferred doneness, place them on a plate and pour the sauce on top.

Nice Girls' Chicken Puttanesca

WASABI PRIME
DUVALL, WASHINGTON
WASABI PRIME
http://wasabiprime.blogspot.com/2010/02/omg-recipe-chicken-puttanesca-making.html

I like to eat. I like to write and photograph. And I like to cook. But really, it's mostly the eating, and I think I'm quite good at that. I am a graphic designer, sharing my time between art and pursuing food writing and photography. I created the blog Wasabi Prime in early 2009 and have been fortunate to have it mentioned in *New York* magazine's "Grub Street" and *Food News Journal*, and the photographs have been featured on TasteSpotting and Serious Eats. My food articles have been published on the *Seattle Post-Intelligencer*, Downtown Bellevue Network, and Bellevue.com. I'm seeing where this path of writing and photography will go, and true to the blog's tagline, I'm taking heaping servings of "food, culture, and whatever else fits on the plate."

SERVES 3

Why do only the naughty ladies of the night get to enjoy a puttanesca sauce? The story behind pasta puttanesca is that it was a simple-to-make sauce comprised of pantry staples, supposedly made by prostitutes between their clients' visits, because of its quick preparation time and inexpensive ingredients. If this is true, I must say the working girls of Italy knew their business, because it's a delicious combination of flavors that makes a good girl wanna go bad. Well, not totally bad—this version of puttanesca has the sauce made with chicken, served over a bed of roasted cauliflower purée; probably a little more involved than the original recipe. We'll just call this one "the Heidi Fleiss of Chicken Puttanesca."

The obvious question is: where the heck's the pasta? I could have made this dish more traditional and made a bed of polenta for the chicken to sit upon, but a purée of cauliflower seemed a more carb-conscious choice, plus I had been looking for a reason to be creative with cauliflower. Cauliflower can often be overlooked, which is a shame, as it's a versatile ingredient, roasts up nicely with a nutty finish, and can be a less starchy and more vitamin-rich alternative to a potato. It's also wicked-cheap at the grocery store and keeps for a while in the crisper drawer of the refrigerator. For the side dish, I removed the green stems of two heads of cauliflower, cut everything down into small, relatively equal-sized pieces, and tossed with oil and herbed salt so they would roast evenly in the oven. A couple of garlic cloves were also added, so they could caramelize. Once softened and slightly browned, everything was promptly buzzed down with some milk and shredded Asiago cheese in a blender. It was easier to keep the consistency loose, so the blender could churn through everything and pour smoothly into the plates.

Yes, there are anchovies in this. Don't be scared. They won't bite; I promise. I was given a little jar of Crown Prince anchovies by a friend, and these little guys really do add a savory, rich flavor to things, whether it's in sauces or something as basic as a chicken Caesar salad. The wee bitty fillets, chopped up small, literally melt into the sauce, giving it a salty richness that's not at all fishy if you're adding just one. Puttanesca sauce traditionally includes these, capers, chopped olives, garlic, and tomatoes. It makes for a perfect "pantry/MacGyver meal," as many of these items are available in most cupboards.

2   boneless, skinless chicken breasts

1   tablespoon butter

Salt and pepper

1   14-ounce can chopped stewed tomatoes

1   cup chopped pitted Kalamata olives

3   cloves garlic, minced

1   whole anchovy fillet, minced

2   teaspoons capers, chopped

¼   cup shredded Asiago or Parmesan cheese to finish

Minced parsley for garnish

1 Split the chicken breasts lengthwise and pound flat, then cut each piece into 3 small pieces. Heat a large pan over medium-high heat and melt the butter. Sprinkle each flattened piece of chicken breast with salt and pepper and cook in batches, browning each side of the chicken until mostly done. Set the chicken aside. Lower the heat to medium and add the tomatoes to deglaze the pan. Use a wooden spoon or spatula to scrape up the brown bits. Reduce the liquid of the tomatoes for 5 to 10 minutes. Stir in the olives, garlic, anchovy, and capers. Stir the sauce for several minutes, letting the liquid continue to reduce.

2 When the sauce is thickened, add the chicken, nestling it into the sauce, and let it sit over low heat for a few minutes to combine the flavors. Sprinkle with the shredded cheese and parsley before serving with a cauliflower purée.

Rack of Lamb with Spicy Fennel Rub

STEPHANIE STIAVETTI
SAN FRANCISCO/OAKLAND, CALIFORNIA
WASABIMON
http://www.wasabimon.com/archive/fennel-rack-of-lamb-recipe/

I'm a food writer living in the San Francisco Bay Area. I particularly love cooking adventurously, taking everyday foods and making them edible by anyone, regardless of dietary restrictions. I do not believe in life without something delicious on the table. Passionate about anything having to do with food or literature, I was fated to combine the two into the makings of a career. After having spent the first half of my adult life submerged in the world of technology, I now make my living as a culinary wordsmith. My work has appeared in such major media outlets as *Pregnancy* magazine, *Clean Eating*, and NPR.com.

SERVES 4

Last week we received a few of our animals from the butcher, so we're swimming in farm-fresh meat here at Chez Wasabimon. Our freezer is packed with a lamb, a goat, half a cow, and another animal that my mother-in-law has sworn me to secrecy over. This rack of lamb recipe is nice and "fennely" with just the right amount of heat. If you like it uber-spicy, feel free to add another chile to the mix or up the amount of black pepper. If you don't know how to french a rack of lamb, it's actually really easy—here's a video to show you how: http://uktv.co.uk/food/stepbystep/aid/53311. If you just can't bring yourself to trim your gorgeous rack, ask your butcher to do it for you. Or better yet, have him show you how so you can do it yourself next time. :)

I like to make broccoli stir-fry in the skillet I used to brown the lamb, making sure to put the "lamby" bits to good use. Heat the pan over medium heat, add ¼ cup of white wine, and scrape loose the meaty bits with a spatula. Toss in 2 tablespoons of olive oil and 2 handfuls of broccoli florets, then stir-fry until the broccoli is bright green and tender but still a little crunchy. This, alongside some brown rice, makes the perfect side for the recipe that follows.

3   tablespoons fennel seeds

½   teaspoon cumin seeds

1   dried red chile

¼   teaspoon ground cardamom

½   teaspoon black or multicolored peppercorns

1   teaspoon sea salt

¼   cup heavy cream or as needed

1   rack of lamb, 8 to 10 ribs, frenched
     and trimmed of all fat

2   tablespoons olive oil

½   teaspoon ground pepper

1   Heat a small skillet over medium heat for 1 minute, then toss in the fennel seeds, cumin seeds, and whole chile. Toast until fragrant, about 2 minutes, agitating every 15 seconds. Remove from the heat and allow to cool.

2   Put the toasted spices into a spice grinder, then add the cardamom, peppercorns, and ½ teaspoon of the salt. Pulse until you have a fine powder, about 30 seconds.

3   Pour the ground spices into a small bowl and add the cream. Mix until you have a paste. Set aside.

4   Split the lamb rack in half so that you have an equal number of ribs in each half. Rub all over with olive oil, then finish up with a rub of the remaining ½ teaspoon salt and the ground pepper.

5   Preheat the oven to 450°F.

6   Heat a heavy skillet over medium heat and sear all sides of the rack, about 2 minutes on each side. Remove from the pan and set in a 9-inch square pan. Let sit until cool enough to touch.

7   Stir the spice paste, which will have thickened up a bit. It should be a spreadable consistency. If it's too thick, add another tablespoon of heavy cream.

8   Spread the spice paste over the meaty parts of the rack and into the cuts between the cutlets. Arrange the racks so that the ribs intertwine, forming an arc.

9   Place the pan in the oven and roast until the internal temperature of the roast is 130°F, 15 to 20 minutes. Remove from the heat and let rest for 10 minutes.

10 Slice the ribs apart and serve.

Rice Noodles with Wonton/Chinese Ravioli in Mushroom Sauce

MY COOKING HUT
LONDON, ENGLAND
MY COOKING HUT
http://www.mycookinghut.com/2008/09/15/rice-noodles-with-wontonchinese-ravioli-in-mushroom-sauce

I come from Malaysia, the country where culinary diversity is found through its multiethnic population of Malay, Indian, Eurasian, Chinese, Nyonya, and the indigenous people of Borneo. I have to say that my upbringing in a multiracial community has great influence in my cooking. Just like any kid, I was pretty quick in picking up new things and tried to remember what I was taught. In Asian kitchens, it is very important to learn basic spices and raw ingredients. For Malaysian Chinese, it's almost compulsory to know how to do proper stir-frying and steaming. With that, it's crucial to learn and master different cutting and chopping styles, which determines the overall look, feel, and taste of the dishes. I make Asian food, mostly Chinese, Malaysian, Indian, Thai, Vietnamese, and Japanese. As my partner is French, I have learned and am still learning to cook classic and modern *délicieux* French food. I do, from time to time, reinvent and create my own recipes.

SERVES 2 TO 4

When I was still at college in Kuala Lumpur, there was this hawker's place I used to go to for noodles. The stall was always packed during lunchtime. Yet so many people didn't mind to queue for the next available table. I was one of them. As I remember, the stall was owned by a Chinese couple. They worked ever so hard to satisfy their patrons' hunger. Their specialty was to serve rice noodles in either mushroom sauce or curry sauce, along with a separate bowl of hot clear soup with wontons. I had never tried mushroom sauce, nor had I tried noodles in curry sauce. I fell in love with both of them and became a regular customer who never failed to visit their stall at least once a week.

Just a few days ago, I had almost an irresistible impulse to creatively re-create and present noodles in mushroom sauce with wonton/Chinese ravioli for my own pleasure. The result satisfied my craving for a taste I had missed for quite a long time. As you may notice, the wonton that I made is a ravioli-like shape.

Slightly less than ½ an 8-ounce packet rice noodles

3   dried shiitake mushrooms, stems discarded

½   carrot, finely chopped

WONTONS:

5   ounces prawns, peeled and minced

3½ ounces pork, minced

    Dash of white pepper

1   tablespoon oyster sauce

1   teaspoon toasted (dark) sesame oil

    Wonton wrappers

MUSHROOM SAUCE:

    Olive or vegetable oil

1   clove garlic, finely chopped

1½ tablespoons oyster sauce

1   tablespoon dark soy sauce

½   cup water

2   teaspoons cornstarch plus 2 tablespoons water

1-inch piece of spring onion, finely sliced lengthwise, for garnish

    Toasted (dark) sesame oil (optional)

1 Soak the rice noodles in warm water for about 20 minutes, until they are soft.

2 In a small bowl, combine the mushroom caps with just enough warm water to soak them until soft. (This water can be incorporated into the recipe and can add a lot of flavor to your dish. Strain it if you wish to use.) Squeeze out the excess water and thinly slice the mushrooms.

3 Put the carrots in a small microwave-safe bowl with a little water. Microwave for 1 to 2 minutes, until crisp-tender. Drain and set aside.

4 To make the wontons, mix all the ingredients except the wonton wrappers in a bowl. Place a wonton skin with one point toward you. Spoon about 1 teaspoon of the filling just off-center on the skin. Fold the bottom point of wonton skin over the filling to make a triangle. Press the edges to seal. Repeat until the filling is used up. Set aside.

5 Heat a pan with some olive or vegetable oil over medium heat. Put in the chopped garlic and cook until almost brown. Put in the sliced shiitake mushrooms and stir for 2 to 3 minutes. Add the oyster and soy sauces and the water.

6 Let the sauce simmer for 10 to 15 minutes.

7 While the mushroom sauce is cooking away, bring a saucepan of water to a boil and cook the wontons in batches. It should take about 5 minutes or less (depending on the size of the filling) for each wonton to cook.

8 Meanwhile, reheat the noodles and arrange the desired portion on each plate.

9 Thicken the sauce with the cornstarch mixture. Spoon a fair amount of sauce over the noodles.

10 Garnish the noodles with the reserved carrots and spring onion. Top the noodles with wontons. Drizzle some sesame oil over the sauce before serving if you wish.

Vietnamese-Style Moo Shu Chive Pancakes with Turkey Leftovers

Vietnamese food is all about the five senses: the visual explosion of colors in green basil and red chiles, the crunching sound of fresh carrots and bean sprouts, aromatic mint and fish sauces, the variety of textures for mouth feel, and . . . oh, yeah, taste is pretty important too. In fact, Vietnamese dishes rarely leave out any part of the tongue with spicy/sweet/tangy mixed with bitter herbs and salty condiments . . . commence Homer Simpson drool . . . NOW.

It seemed a natural progression for leftover turkey or any roast fowl. Turkey not being the most flavorful of meats on its own, the kick of some cilantro and ginger sounded pretty good. Since the leftover meat is easiest to remove from the carcass in shreds, I also thought some moo shu would work, and that would mean pancakes.

I found the basic pancake recipe from Emeril Lagasse, and I must not've read through it properly the first time, because I didn't realize I was essentially making pastry dough pancakes. If I'd known that before making them, I probably would've closed the page and looked for something else to make. Why? Because I'm afraid of pastry dough. Everyone makes it sound like some huge ordeal of rolling and buttering and layering. As someone who cooks way more than bakes, I just imagined myself collapsing in a tearful mess about halfway through, covered in flour with bits of dough mashed into my hair. I'm wearing a chef's hat in this dream sequence, and it's slumped in defeat, too . . .

I'm glad I didn't read the recipe through properly as it turns out. By the time I got to the layering part, I was having too much fun to care. I was giddy with the realization that this was far from

MATHEA TANNER
CHICAGO, ILLINOIS
PEAS LOVE CARROTS
http://peaslovecarrots.blogspot.com/2009/11/
vietnamese-style-moo-shu-pancakes-mu-xu.html

I love food and Muppets.

SERVES 6, 2 PANCAKES EACH

"work"; I was humming while rolling out little disks, brushing them with sesame oil, and sticking some chives in between the layers . . . then a little sizzle on the griddle pan and there they were! For my filling I used some leftovers from the original dinner: onions and yellow heirloom carrots, even Brussels sprouts. I added cilantro on the side and made a chili/garlic sauce for dipping. Since the recipe is designed to be a vehicle for tasty leftover turkey dinners, I didn't include a set-in-stone ingredient list for the filling—more of a formula. The results are a five-sense explosion you don't get in a typical turkey.

PANCAKES:

1½ cups all-purpose flour, plus a little extra for rolling

   Pinch of salt

½ cup boiling water

3 tablespoons sesame oil

   A few chives, coarsely chopped

TURKEY FILLING:

2 tablespoons toasted sesame oil

1 cup each shredded raw carrots, cabbage, and mushrooms

½ cup chopped green onions or other onions

3 cups shredded cooked turkey

1 teaspoon grated peeled fresh ginger

3 cloves garlic, crushed

3 tablespoons soy sauce

2 tablespoons brown sugar

½ teaspoon fish sauce

 Salt and pepper

1 egg, beaten

CHILI/GARLIC SAUCE:

3 tablespoons toasted sesame oil

1 tablespoon red chili sauce (such as sambal oelek or Sriracha)

1 clove garlic, crushed

1 teaspoon grated peeled fresh ginger

GARNISH:

 Several sprigs fresh mint, Thai basil, and cilantro

 Fresh bean sprouts

 Shredded carrots

 Lime wedges

 Crushed peanuts

1 To make the pancakes, combine the flour, salt, and boiling water in a medium bowl, stirring with a heatproof spoon (whisks get gummy; not recommended). Add cold water 1 tablespoon at a time and stir until you have a slightly sticky dough—you may need up to 3 tablespoons.

2 Turn the dough out onto a floured surface and knead for 10 minutes, until smooth. Cover and let rest for 30 minutes.

3 Divide your dough in half, roll each half into a ball, and divide each into sixths. You should have 12 pieces.

4 Roll each piece into a ball between the palms of your hands. Using a rolling pin on a lightly floured surface, roll out each ball into a 2-inch disk. Stack the disks in pairs, brushing some sesame oil and sprinkling a few chopped chives in between the 2 disks. Roll out your disk "sandwiches" into 7- to 8-inch pancakes.

5 Heat a heavy skillet or griddle over medium-high heat, brush lightly with sesame oil, and add pancakes one at a time. Cook on both sides until blistered but not browned. There will be several air pockets. Set aside the finished pancakes, covered, to keep them warm.

6 To make the turkey filling, heat 2 tablespoons sesame oil in a wok or medium skillet. Add the vegetables and onions, adding those with longer cooking times first. Cook until tender but still crisp. Add your cooked shredded meat, plus the ginger, garlic, soy, brown sugar, fish sauce, and salt and pepper to taste. Add your beaten egg and toss/stir.

7 Heat until everything is heated thoroughly and the egg is cooked, about 2 minutes.

8 For the chili sauce, mix all the ingredients together in a bowl until incorporated.

9 Serve the pancakes with bowls of the filling and garnishes. Let your guests fill and roll their own pancakes and garnish as desired.

Baked Lentil Cheeseburgers

ELYSE EISENBERG
NEW YORK, NY
CREATIVE DELITES
http://creativedelites.com/2010/01/18/baked-lentil-
veggie-burgers

SERVES 4

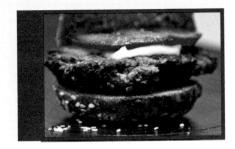

Leave your preconceptions at the door and try this simply delicious veggie burger recipe. In a world where "veggie burger" means a flattened block of soy protein, studded with carrots and peas whose flavor is thankfully masked with ketchup, mustard, and lots of relish, it doesn't take a lot to build a better burger. All you really need to make a delicious, homemade burger is a can of beans, some eggs, and rolled oats or bread crumbs. The good news is that you probably have most, if not all, of these ingredients at home. Add some different spices and fresh herbs, and the burgers can be flavored in a variety of ways. My favorite one starts with lentils, fresh cilantro, and ginger and is topped with melted Jarlsberg cheese. If you are looking for more ingredient and preparation ideas for burgers, check out a recent blog post in the *New York Times*, "The Burger Experience without Beef."

BURGER:

1   14-ounce can lentils, drained (feel free to
     use a different kind of cooked bean)

1   medium onion, diced

1   cup rolled oats

1   egg

1   teaspoon crushed peeled fresh ginger

1   teaspoon chopped cilantro

1   teaspoon chili powder (less or more,
     depending on how spicy you want it)

½   teaspoon garam masala

1   teaspoon salt (less or more, depending
     on how salty you want it)

     Freshly ground black pepper

1   teaspoon raw or brown sugar

TOPPINGS:

4   onion sandwich rolls

4   slices regular or light Jarlsberg cheese

1   tomato, sliced

     Black sesame seeds

1 Preheat the oven to 425°F and spray a baking sheet with grape-
       seed or any neutral oil.

2 Combine the lentils, onion, oats, egg, ginger, cilantro, spices,
       salt, pepper, and sugar in a food processor and pulse until
       chunky. You want a mixture that is moist but not wet.

3 Let the mixture rest for a few minutes, then shape into 4 patties.

4 Bake the burgers until they are deeply browned, 8 to 10 min-
       utes. Then flip and bake for 8 to 10 minutes longer.

5 Toast the onion rolls and serve each burger on a toasted roll.
       Top with Jarlsberg cheese and sliced tomato and sprinkle with
       the sesame seeds.

4 Side Dishes

Ancient Grains Bread

SARAH REID
OSHAWA, ONTARIO, CANADA
WHAT SMELLS . . . SO GOOD?
http://yummysmells.blogspot.com/2009/12/ancient-grain-modern-twist.html

I'm a nutrition student with a passion for reinstilling the love of good-quality, homemade, and mostly healthy food in the hearts and kitchens of children and their families today. I believe that all foods made in the home, even when labeled as "naughty," are more wholesome treats than prepackaged, cookie-cutter junk. I'll bake anything and everything, so long as there's someone to eat it!

MAKES 1 LOAF

One of the great things I've recently enjoyed sharing is my love of making homemade breads. It's nothing new on my blog for sure, but to most people the art of making bread regularly at home is an archaic, and sadly lost, tradition. But what better way to share the decadence of these tiny, new-yet-old grains?

1 envelope instant dry yeast

2¼ cups all-purpose flour

1 cup whole wheat flour

⅓ cup rye flakes

3 tablespoons ground flaxseed

3 tablespoons amaranth grain

⅓ cup quinoa

¼ cup soy flour

1½ tablespoons vital wheat gluten

⅓ cup skim milk powder

½ teaspoon salt

1⅓ cups warm water

¼ cup honey

1. In a large bowl or stand mixer, whisk together the yeast, flours, rye flakes, flaxseed, amaranth, quinoa, soy flour, wheat gluten, skim milk powder, and salt.

2. Stir in the warm water and honey, mixing thoroughly to form a cohesive, fairly firm (but workable) dough. Turn out onto a floured board or knead with the dough hook in a stand mixer for 12 minutes, until very elastic and smooth. Place in a bowl, cover, and allow to rest 30 minutes.

3. Roll the rested dough into a log shape and tuck into a greased 9 by 5-inch loaf pan. Cover with a clean towel and allow to rise for 50 to 60 minutes.

4. Preheat the oven to 350°F. Slash the top of the loaf 2 or 3 times with a sharp knife before placing in the oven.

5. Bake for 40 minutes, or until golden brown. Turn out of the pan immediately and cool on a rack before slicing.

Gluten-Free Onion Rings

JEANINE FRIESEN
MANITOBA, CANADA
THE BAKING BEAUTIES
http://www.thebakingbeauties.com/2009/10/gluten-free-onion-rings.html

I live in rural Manitoba with my husband (the writer) of eleven years and our two wonderful children, the Princess (seven) and the Pirate (four). I enjoy working in the kitchen, although I have been known to let the dishes pile up.

SERVES 4

Onion rings and I go way back. I remember being a small child in the backseat of my parents' lime-green two-door Nova, sitting in the parking lot of the A&W waiting for the carhops to bring our food. I always had onion rings and a small root beer. I remember my brother telling me that onion rings had onions in them. No . . . no, they didn't. I like onion rings, but I hate onions. They can't have onions in them. Well, twenty-five-plus years later I'll admit it: onion rings do indeed have onions in them. :) The smell of onion rings frying as you walk past the fast-food joints calls you in. But since celiac disease has made its appearance the kids are enjoying the onion rings and Mom's always got to pass them by. So, the challenge was posed: I would make my own onion rings at home! These were really delicious, and after doing a taste test with white, yellow, and red onions, our family agreed . . . yellow was the way to go. These onion rings are really great right out of the fryer, but for some reason they get soggier when you have them in the oven for too long. So, it's best to eat them right away.

1	egg
¼	cup vegetable oil
1	cup milk
1½	cups gluten-free all-purpose flour
½	teaspoon salt
1	teaspoon baking powder
2	large yellow onions, sliced and separated into rings
	Canola oil for deep frying

1 In a medium bowl, mix the egg, oil, and milk on low speed with a mixer for 1 minute. Add 1 cup of the flour, the salt and the baking powder; mix until smooth.

2 Put the remaining ½ cup flour in a separate small bowl.

3 Heat at least 1 inch of oil to 375°F.

4 Coat the onions in the flour, then dip in the batter. Gently drop the battered rings into the hot oil and fry until the desired shade of brown.

Cannellini Beans with Fennel, Red Onion, and Saffron

DEBORAH CHUD
CHESTNUT HILL, MA
A DOCTOR'S KITCHEN: RECIPE OF THE WEEK AND ODDS & ENDS
http://www.adoctorskitchen.com/archives/cannellini-beans-with-fennel-red-onion-and-saffron-2

I'm a physician and food writer, but I think of myself as a healthy food strategist. I've spent my entire adult life developing ways to make conventional food healthier and healthy food taste better. I inherited my passion for food from my paternal grandmother—a professional chef and caterer who opened her own restaurant on Miami Beach in 1936. My father, her son, was a gifted amateur chef, and our house was full of great smells, tastes, and intense talk about food. My cookbook, *The Gourmet Prescription*, was published in 1996. I am currently a food columnist for *Radius* magazine, a national lifestyle quarterly devoted to health and wellness that circulates to physicians and waiting rooms throughout the country.

SERVES 6 TO 8

I hate canned beans. Don't get me wrong: I'm all for speed and convenience, but some things just can't be rushed. Compared to their poor canned relations, home-cooked beans have much more flavor, better texture, and a lower glycemic index. While the starchy, viscous medium that surrounds canned beans is best rinsed off, the delicate cooking liquid in your own bean pot is eminently usable—as a soup base or a moistening agent for a bean stew. As far as convenience goes, I cook mine when life permits. Beans demand time but no labor, so they're prime candidates for multitasking. I make them on Sunday afternoons while I do laundry, return e-mails, and pay bills. All you need is a block of time when you're going to be around.

¼   teaspoon saffron threads

2   tablespoons boiling water

1   tablespoon extra virgin olive oil

1   cup chopped fennel bulb, fronds reserved

½   cup chopped red onion

3   cups cooked cannellini beans, with
the liquid that clings to them

Salt and freshly ground black pepper

Bean-cooking liquid or vegetable broth as needed

Minced flat-leaf parsley or chopped
fennel fronds, for garnish

1 Combine the saffron and boiling water in a small heatproof bowl or measuring cup; set aside for 5 minutes.

2 Heat the oil in large nonstick skillet; add the fennel and onion. Cook, stirring occasionally, until tender, about 5 minutes.

3 Add the beans and the saffron mixture to the skillet and stir to blend. Season to taste with salt and pepper. If the mixture seems dry, add some of the bean-cooking liquid or vegetable broth to achieve your desired consistency. Sprinkle with parsley or fennel fronds and serve immediately.

Crispy Latkes

MAYA ROOK
ALBANY, NEW YORK
A SLICE OF EARTHLY DELIGHT
http://sliceofearthlydelight.blogspot.com/2009/12/celebrating-with-latkes.html

SERVES 2

Food is an incredibly valuable tool for learning about other cultures, religions, and traditions. It helps us understand how other people see the world and live their lives. With the holiday of Chanukah occurring right now, cooking and eating traditional Chanukah foods is a way to experience others' culture if you are not Jewish and to immerse yourself further in your heritage if you are Jewish. While in elementary school, the parents of Jewish families would always come in during Chanukah and teach the class about the holiday and teach us to make latkes. Coming from a Buddhist family and living in a largely Christian town, the experience of learning about Jewish traditions in school informed me about other people's beliefs and traditional holiday practices. Today, many schools choose to ignore religion altogether, but I have to say that learning about Chanukah in school certainly opened me up to other experiences and also made me feel more connected to the traditions being celebrated at my friends' homes. And I really can't argue with using food to teach children about anything!

Potatoes made crispy by frying in oil always taste good, and I'm a big fan of fries and chips—but latkes are really something special. You don't have latkes just any old day. Those lovely potato pancakes that are crispy on the outside and slightly soft on the inside, nice and warm, topped with sour cream and applesauce, are a treat that don't come too often throughout the year. In celebration of Chanukah, latkes, and other fried foods, symbolize the oil that lasted for eight days in the Temple in Jerusalem. The story behind the holiday is that the Syrians were driven out of Israel by Judah and his followers, called the Maccabees, and the Temple in Jerusalem was reclaimed. After the temple was rededicated, the Maccabees wanted to light the N'er Tamid, or eternal light, which once lit should not be extinguished, but they had only enough oil for the light to burn for one night. They found a small amount of oil to light the lamp that was enough to burn for one evening but miraculously lasted for eight nights, which was enough time to process more oil to keep the lamp lit. Today those of the Jewish faith celebrate this Festival of Lights by lighting a menorah each night for eight nights, exchanging gifts, and eating celebratory foods like latkes.

2	large baking potatoes
½	white onion
1	tablespoon all-purpose flour or matzo meal
1	egg
	Salt
	Vegetable oil

1. Peel and grate the potatoes and dice the onion.

2. Place the grated potatoes and diced onion on a paper towel or dry cloth. Roll the towel up around the potatoes and onion and squeeze to remove any excess moisture. This step will help keep the latkes crispy while you fry them.

3. Put the potato and onion in a bowl and add the flour, egg, and a little bit of salt. Mix together.

4. Heat the vegetable oil in a frying pan or skillet over medium-high heat. Place spoonfuls (about 2 tablespoons) of the batter into the hot oil and push them down to form flat pancakes. Fry for a few minutes on each side, until golden brown.

5. Remove from the oil with a slotted spoon and place the latkes on a rack with paper towel underneath so any extra oil can drip off. Sprinkle them with salt to taste. If you need to keep the latkes warm, place them in a warm oven while you finish making the rest of the batch.

6. Serve with sides of sour cream and applesauce.

East Indian Potato Chops

Potato chops, an East Indian specialty of mashed potato stuffed with delicately spiced minced beef, is one of my mother's signature dishes. As I currently live abroad in Dubai, UAE, it is often one of the first things I request my mother make when I return home on vacation to Bombay, India. One of the best memories my sister and I have is of my mother using these as a weapon against my father when they had just had a fight. Since they usually did not speak to each other during their fights my father refused to eat any food prepared by my mother and would resort to cooking his own meals. However, when the "cold war" went on for more than a day or two, my mother would turn to making potato chops to put an end to it. And they are one thing my father couldn't resist—yes, the chops are that good. Of course, my father wouldn't touch any of them during the day when they were just prepared. After my mum had packed them away for the night, he would have a midnight feast. The next day my mother would check the storage container and triumphantly take note that there were a couple missing. And that was the truce. When they faced each other that day, they would smile, kiss, and make up.

I recently found a recipe for Kubbat Potato in *The Iraqi Cookbook* by Lamees Ibrahim. The recipe was similar to the way my mother makes the potato chops, except for the use of parsley and the addition of flaked almonds. The biggest question I had was "Had we East Indians borrowed it from them, or were they inspired by us?" Either way, here's my mother's recipe, which I have finally learnt to make after years of watching her and complaining it is too tedious. Now I just have to get my own husband addicted to them.

BEVERLEY ANN D'CRUZ
MISSISSAUGA, ONTARIO, CANADA
POTATO CHOPS AND BONELESS CHICKEN
http://potatochopsandbonelesschix.blogspot.com/
search/label/potato%20chops

An amateur cook's journey discovering foods of my culture (and the rest of the world) and the healing power of nutritious food as a caregiver to a brain tumour survivor—my husband.

14 DEPENDING ON SIZE

Vegetable oil

4   large onions, finely chopped

1   inch fresh ginger, peeled and finely chopped

6   cloves garlic, finely chopped

2   green chiles, seeded and finely chopped

½   pound ground beef

Salt and pepper

2   tablespoons finely chopped cilantro

1   tablespoon finely chopped fresh mint

Juice of 1 lime

2¼ cups salted mashed potatoes

1   egg, lightly beaten

Bread crumbs

1   Heat 1 teaspoon oil in a frying pan and add the onions. Sauté over medium heat until lightly caramelised.

2   Then add the ginger, garlic, and green chiles and continue to fry the mixture until fragrant, 2 to 3 minutes.

3   Turn up the heat to medium-high, add the ground beef, and season with salt and pepper. Sauté until lightly browned. Lower the heat and continue to cook the meat until all the liquid has evaporated. When cooked through, remove from the heat and toss with the herbs and lime juice. Set aside to cool until needed.

4   Take a portion of the cooled mashed potato (about the size of a Ping-Pong ball) and flatten it to form the shape of your palm (it should be about ¼ inch thick). If the potato is too sticky, grease your palm with some oil. Cup your palm a little to form a pocket.

5   Add 1½ tablespoons of the cooled meat mixture to the centre of the flattened potato pocket. Enclose the filling by drawing up the sides of the potato and cover the filling completely so no meat is visible. Continue with the rest of the mashed potato and meat.

6   Heat a generous amount of oil in a wide frying pan. One by one, roll each of the potato chops in egg, then coat them with bread crumbs.

7   Place in the frying pan and cook until each potato chop is golden brown. Serve hot with a side salad or homemade chili sauce.

Farro with Mushrooms and Asparagus

KAROLINE BOEHM-GOODNICK
SAN FRANCISCO, CALIFORNIA
SWEET KAROLINE
http://sweetkarolineadventuresinfood.blogspot.
com/2009/11/little-something-to-wet-your-appetite.
html

I am a freelance writer and baker living in San Francisco. I have also worked as a cook, pastry chef, wine steward, waitress, cocktail server, hostess, FOH manager, photographer, and stylist. I love food and anything else that one puts in the mouth to provide nourishment, calories, or sedation.

SERVES 4

Meredith Berger, nutrition intern at Emerson Hospital, says, "Whenever I make a grain dish, I try to beef it up with some finely chopped vegetables to make the grain portion size smaller but be just as filling." In this case, farro, rated medium on the glycemic index (GI), is beefed up with asparagus and mushrooms. The addition of protein-rich chicken stock and sherry vinegar lowers the overall GI of the dish. The cereal is an ancient cousin to modern-day wheat and sometimes known as emmer wheat. High in B vitamins but low in gluten, it may be tolerated by some with wheat allergies. Choose the semipearled version, as it cooks faster than the whole grain. Farro is often cooked like rice or pasta. For this recipe, boil the kernels first and then transfer to a skillet to absorb the flavors of the sauce. To make the dish vegetarian, soak the mushrooms in 2 cups of water; reserve it and use in place of chicken stock.

1   ounce dried mushrooms

8   ounces semipearled farro

1   tablespoon olive oil

1   medium onion, chopped

2   cloves garlic, minced

1   tablespoon chopped fresh thyme

3   tablespoons sherry vinegar

2   cups chicken stock

1   bunch asparagus, cut into ¼-inch pieces

    Salt and pepper

1 In a small bowl, cover the dried mushrooms with warm water. Soak for 25 minutes, or until softened.

2 Drain the mushrooms and discard the soaking water. Chop fine.

3 Bring a large pot of water to a boil. Add the farro and cook for 10 minutes, stirring occasionally. Drain and reserve.

4 In a large skillet over medium heat, heat the olive oil and add the onion, garlic, thyme, and mushrooms. Cook, stirring occasionally, for 5 minutes, or until the onion is tender.

5 Stir in 2 tablespoons of the sherry vinegar and continue cooking for 1 minute. Add the chicken stock and bring it to a boil. Stir in the reserved farro and return to a boil. Lower the heat to a simmer and cover with a tight-fitting lid. Cook for 10 minutes. Add the asparagus and cook, covered, for 10 minutes.

6 Season with the remaining 1 tablespoon sherry vinegar and salt and pepper to taste.

My Grandmother's Migas

MIRIAM
GALAPAGAR, SPAIN
THE WINTER GUEST: THE WORLD SEEN FROM
MY KITCHEN
http://invitadoinviernoeng.blogspot.com/2009/11/
my-grandmothers-migas.html

I'm an English-Spanish translator, with a chemistry background, obsessed with food and cooking . . . and some other things. I have a partner who witnesses undisturbed how I stuff the house with loads of kitchen gadgets and artifacts and mountains of cookbooks. I'm also a mother of two boys who don't care for my cooking at all. Too bad for them! But still I've got some hope.

SERVES 8

First of all, I shall explain what *migas* are. In Spanish, *migas* literally means "crumbs." To prepare them you just need a hunk of stale bread, some charcuterie, cloves of garlic, and olive oil for frying. It was formerly shepherd's fare, something easy to prepare for the shepherds while up on the mountains and also popular among peasants. Everybody had a piece of bread and some garlic and chorizo or ham to add. Apparently there is a version of *migas* in every region of Spain.

I warn you: this is not a diet dish. It has lots of olive oil and animal fats, and I won't apologize for that—that's why it's so delicious. It was perfect for warming you up on the cold winter nights up in a mountain hut. It was my grandmother María who taught me to make *migas*. She was my paternal grandmother, who lived with my family till her death, some twenty years ago.

As far as I know there are two main types of *migas*: diced and pulled. My grandmother used to make the diced type. According to the traditional standards, the dices must be chickpea sized. The best bread for *migas* is the Spanish peasant bread with a very dense crumb. The very open crumb of baguette or ciabatta are not good for *migas*. Normally, day- or two-old stale bread is used. Remember, *migas* is a poor man's dish . . . this makes it just perfect for the current economic crisis.

1   hunk of dense crumb stale bread, diced in chick pea–sized pieces (about 2 cups)

1   teaspoon salt

2   teaspoons sweet Spanish pimentón (paprika)

6 to 8 tablespoons extra virgin olive oil

4   cloves garlic

2   chorizos, diced (a type that is not too dry—not all chorizos are good for frying; about 1 cup)

2   tablespoons diced Spanish jamón

4 to 5 strips of bacon, diced

1 Put the diced bread in a large bowl. Then sprinkle the bread with enough water to moisten it slightly.

2 Sprinkle with the salt and toss the bread to distribute the salt evenly. Do the same with the pimentón. Then cover with a damp cloth and leave to rest overnight.

3 The next day, pour the olive oil into a deep frying pan and put it over medium heat.

4 Cut the garlic cloves in half without peeling and fry until lightly browned, just to flavor the oil, then discard the garlic.

5 Add the chorizo, ham, and, bacon. Fry until almost done. Add the cubed bread and toss and turn it around until it thoroughly soaks up the oil.

6 Continue tossing for 3 to 4 minutes over medium heat. The *migas* should be lightly toasted and crisp on the outside, while they should remain soft on the inside. Yes, that's the key to making good *migas*, my little children.

7 Serve the *migas* warm on a beautiful earthenware dish and distribute them with a large wooden spoon. You can add some grapes to the *migas* too, although I don't remember my grandmother doing it. This was very typical in the wine-growing regions, where they are called *migas de vendimia*, or "grape harvest *migas*." I love the contrast between the roughness of the *migas* and the sweetness of the grapes. Or serve the *migas* in small bowls or portions for a very tasty tapa.

KATE
LOS ANGELES, CALIFORNIA
SAVOUR FARE
http://savour-fare.com/2009/07/28/jammin-plum-jam/

Savour Fare is a website featuring recipes, reviews, and content aimed toward the home cook. It is produced and written by me, a working mother based in Los Angeles. Savour Fare focuses primarily on recipes that are accessible, easy, and delicious and aims through recipes, tutorials, and reviews to take the mystique out of cooking good food, every day.

MAKES 4 HALF-PINT JARS

Plum Jam

I have a confession to make. I have been cooking this summer, but not dinner, and not dessert. I have been making jam. There's something special about those little jars of homemade preserves, all lined up, ready to be eaten, or given away as gifts, or, if you have a packrat nature (like nobody I know, nosirree) to be stored in the pantry and gazed at lovingly. My husband makes fun of me, pointing out that I have an Ivy League education, am admitted to the Bar in two states, have a successful career, and yet I am proud of making jam, something his great-grandmother did on a regular basis without much fuss. So sue me. I'm proud of my jam. I love my jam. I bid thee to go forth and make your own jam. You won't be sorry. There are two parts to canning jam, both of which can be intimidating—the cooking of the jam and the canning for preservation. On the first point, here are a few tips: Use the peels of the fruit—they tend to have higher pectin (the stuff that makes the jam jammy, rather than syrupy). Cook it longer than you might think (it's really just candy; use a candy thermometer to 220°F or cook until it starts to firm up on a cool dish). And use commercial pectin if you're either using a low-pectin fruit (like rhubarb) or worried about the jam factor (I don't mind if my jam is a little runny, myself). On the canning part, calm down! I know there are a million botulism horror stories out there, but jam has a slightly higher margin of error since it is so acidic and so sugary, both of which help preserve the jam and make it less susceptible to bacteria. Also, the process really isn't difficult, though it helps to have a few good tools, like good tongs and a rack that fits inside your biggest pot. I found a canning kit at Amazon to be reasonably priced and very useful, and the rack fits perfectly into my 8-quart stockpot.

I've found a good rule of thumb is that a pound of fruit makes about one jar of jam, and I tend to make no more than four at a time. I also like to make jam that's harder to buy in the stores—the recipe below is for plum jam, which is unutterably delicious but nearly impossible to find at the A&P. If this is too much for you, you can just make the jam and keep it in your refrigerator. If you can it, you can save it forever and ever and pull it out of the pantry periodically to gloat over. What? Doesn't everyone do that with jam? It's also excellent on toast, over some Greek yogurt, stirred into oatmeal, or filling a crêpe. The only problem is that once you start making jam, you'll probably be hard-pressed to stop. My pantry is getting full. But at least I can make it through the winter.

3   pounds prune plums, pitted and roughly chopped

1   pound granulated sugar

1 Combine the unpeeled fruit and the sugar in a large pot and cook over medium heat, stirring frequently, until the mixture starts to resemble jam—i.e., when you drag a spoon or a spatula along the bottom of the pot, the separation remains for a bit before the syrup fills it in (this should be about 220°F on a candy thermometer, but it's OK if you're a little on the low side).

2 Meanwhile, sterilize those little half-pint jars with the lids and the separate rings and pop them into boiling water for at least 10 minutes. You can just leave them in there while you're cooking the jam.

3 Fill the hot jars with hot jam, leaving ¼ inch of space, wipe the rims with a clean damp towel, then put on the lids and the rings. Return the sealed jars to the boiling water for another 10 minutes. The jars shouldn't touch the bottom of your pan, which is why a canning rack comes in useful, and the water should cover the jars.

4 Remove the jars from the hot water and let cool overnight. The lids should seal as the jam cools—you may even hear an audible pop.

5 Once the jars are cool, remove the rings for storage.

Spinach Coriander Chive Bread

VEGGI FARE
MUNICH, BAVARIA, GERMANY
VEGGIE FARE. FROM HERE AND THERE . . .
http://rachanakothari.blogspot.com/2009/12/having-widened-my-horizons-from-eating.html

I am originally from Kolkata, India, and currently living in Munich, Germany, with my husband. My recipes come from the beautiful places I visit, the wonderful people I come across, and especially from my mother-in-law and my mom. Lot of these recipes are a result of experimenting with variations on traditional recipes.

MAKES 4 SMALL BUNS

Having widened my horizons from eating just white toast bread until a couple of years ago, to the wonderful wide world of the almost endless varieties of this very versatile staple, all the way to starting to bake bread myself a few months ago, I'm pretty new to the bread-baking business. However, after starting late, I have caught on with fervor and love trying out new variations. Whenever I bake bread, and see it rising in the oven, my heart does a little tap dance and a smile visits my face. I started with standard bread recipes, and this was the first of my own variations. It turned out to be a hit with the neighbours and my hubby, and I hope you like it too!

½ cup plus 2 tablespoons very warm, but not hot, low-fat milk, plus more to brush on the bread

½ teaspoon sugar

1 teaspoon active dry yeast

¾ cup all-purpose flour, plus more as needed

¾ cup whole wheat flour

¾ teaspoon salt

2 tablespoons finely chopped chives

2 tablespoons finely chopped coriander leaves

3 tablespoons shredded fresh spinach, stems removed

1½ tablespoons sunflower oil

A few assorted seeds to sprinkle on the bread (pumpkin, sesame, sunflower, etc.)

1 Preheat the oven to 400°F and grease a baking sheet.

2 Place the warm milk, sugar, and yeast in a bowl. Mix well and leave in a warm place until frothy, 10 to 15 minutes.

3 Sift the flours and salt into a bowl. Then add the chives, coriander leaves, and spinach. Rub in the oil until the mixture resembles fine bread crumbs.

4 Add the yeast mixture to the flour and mix to form a soft but manageable dough (add 1 tablespoon of all-purpose flour at a time if the dough is too sticky, but avoid adding too much flour).

5 Place the dough in an oiled bowl, cover with plastic wrap, and leave to rise in a warm place until double in size, about an hour.

6 Turn out onto a floured surface, knead lightly, and shape the dough into 4 small rolls. Allow the rolls to rest on a greased baking sheet, covered loosely with plastic wrap, and leave to rise in a warm place until they double in size.

7 Remove the plastic wrap. Brush the tops of the loaves with some milk and sprinkle on the seeds. Bake in the preheated oven for 15 to 20 minutes.

8 Allow to cool completely on a wire rack.

5 Desserts

"Orangette" Tea Sandwiches

BRITTAN HELLER
GROTON, VERMONT
THE SUITCASE CHEF
http://www.thesuitcasechef.com/exotic-edibles-hallabong-or-dekopan-or-shiranui

I'm an international human rights lawyer who loves learning about new cultures and cuisines. My work has taken me almost everywhere, so I've been lucky enough to have eaten my way around the world. My blog presents unusual local foods I've encountered along the way, original creations inspired by the places I've been, and food news and views that encourage me to eat mindfully.

SERVES 4

Today I brought home a new fruit. New fruit days are exciting! Romanized it is called a *hallabong*. It was softball sized and orange like a Halloween pumpkin. Unlike other citrus fruits I've found, it had a characteristic bump at the top, very thick skin, and no seeds. The taste was a pleasing combination of mild grapefruit and tangerine. It looked like it would smell wonderful, but my hallabong had no scent. However, what it lacked in odor it made up for in beauty.

Hallabong fruits are very expensive in Korea. Typically, a flat of eight or so perfect fruits will be sold for roughly $20. The fruit is given as a present for Lunar New Year, Chusok (Korean Thanksgiving), or one's birthday. Mine had made their way from the flat into the grocer's case because they were slightly imperfect (thus making them perfectly affordable). The word *hallabong* describes the region where these fruit come from in Korea. Hallasan is a mountain on Jeju Island, a southern honeymooners' paradise where tangerines, green tea—and *hallabongs*—are cultivated. The bump at the top is supposed to resemble this mountain. The *hallabong* originated as a hybrid fruit in Japan. There it is called a *dekopon* and generically known as *shiranui* (不知火). *Dekopon* describes both the bump on the top (deko-) and one of the two citrus fruits that were crossed to create it: a *kiyomi*, a satsuma hybrid; and the *pon-kan*, a tangerine with orange-sized fruit. Basically, in family reunion language, it's a tangerine twice removed.

We enjoyed the *hallabongs* for breakfast with plain yogurt. They needed nothing else. However, if you're feeling creative, try these orange curd paninis—they taste like orangettes (candied orange peel dipped in chocolate)!

½ to ¾ cup fresh hallabong juice (use a mixture of fresh tangerine and fresh orange juice if unavailable)

Grated zest of 1 orange

1 tablespoon lemon juice

¼ cup sugar

1 large egg

2 large egg yolks

Pinch of salt

4 tablespoons (½ stick) unsalted butter, cut into chunks and softened, plus 1 tablespoon for cooking the sandwiches

¼ cup Nutella

4 slices soft white sandwich bread

1 First make the *hallabong* curd. Reduce the *hallabong* juice to ¼ cup in a medium saucepan over medium heat, 3 to 5 minutes. Pour it into a measuring cup to cool and add the orange zest and lemon juice.

2 In a medium bowl, whisk together the sugar, egg, egg yolks, and salt. When the *hallabong* reduction has cooled to room temperature, whisk it into the egg mixture in a steady stream.

3 Return the egg mixture to the saucepan. Cook over medium-low heat, whisking constantly, until the mixture thickens to a pudding-like thickness. It's done when you are able to lift the whisk from the pan and the curd holds its shape when it falls back into the saucepan. This should take 6 to 8 minutes, and the curd should reach 180°F.

4 Remove from the heat. For a smooth curd, press it through a strainer, or skip this step and leave the zest in for a stronger flavor. Stir in 4 tablespoons butter until well combined.

5 Store the hallabong curd in the refrigerator until cool. Place a sheet of plastic wrap over the top so it doesn't get a weird rubbery skin.

6 Next, make a panino with the Nutella and *hallabong* curd: Spread about 1 tablespoon Nutella and 1 tablespoon *hallabong* curd on a slice of bread. More can be added to your taste preferences. Top with the other slice of bread.

7 Make your panini in a Foreman Grill or a sandwich press for the greatest ease and crunch. Alternatively, place the remaining tablespoon of butter in a skillet over medium heat and swirl to coat the pan. When the butter ceases foaming, place your sandwich in the skillet. Weigh down the sandwich with a heavy small pan, if you wish, to make it more panino-like. Flip the sandwich when the bottom is golden brown. Remove from the heat when the bottom is crunchy and golden brown.

8 Cut into quarters and serve while warm. Enjoy for teatime or as a rich breakfast. A vanilla tea like Mariage Frères Bourbon Vanilla or a good Earl Grey goes wonderfully with the citrus and chocolate notes.

Apple Pie Bars

THE RUNAWAY SPOON
MEMPHIS, TENNESSEE
THE RUNAWAY SPOON
http://therunawayspoon.com/blog/2009/09/the-apple-doesnt-fall-far-from-the-tree

I think I am like most people, somewhere in the middle between food snob and food schlub. Sometimes I pull out all the stops; sometimes speed and convenience win out.

MAKES 24 BARS

Once upon a time there was a beautiful apple tree. When I was maybe ten, my dad took me to the plant nursery and let me choose whatever kind of tree I wanted to plant in the backyard, to replace one that had died. My family had just enjoyed some magnificent apples, bright red with little red capillary-like veins running through the creamy white flesh. At the market they were labeled Rome Beauty, at a time when the choice was usually just red or green. Thirty years later I still remember those apples. No Rome Beauty I have ever purchased has had those little veins. But I was so intrigued by that delicious apple that when apple varieties were an option for the new tree, I had to have one. So the tree was planted overhanging the patio and grew there slowly, doing little more than casting shade. But it was my and Daddy's tree.

About ten years ago, the tree started to produce apples. Little, hard green ones at first, most of which fell to the ground or were eaten by birds, but eventually my farmer father rigged up some netting, and the apples proliferated. Apples, apples everywhere! My father even jerry-rigged this little bag-on-a-stick thingy to harvest the apples from the high branches. By the time the tree started producing apples, I was no longer living at home. So the task of dealing with the apples fell to my mother, and she took to it like a champion. She collected apple cookbooks, cut out every magazine recipe involving apples, and copied down anything friends passed along. She still has a red file folder stuffed with apple ideas. She makes amazing apple sauce and apple bread. She peels and cuts the apples and dips them in acidulated water, then freezes plastic bags full so we can have fresh applesauce anytime. And she makes amazing apple pie. She freezes those too, so we always have one at family get-togethers.

Apples became a great gift-giving theme, which I imagine she hated. For Christmas and birthdays we gave her apple peelers, apple pie dishes, apple books, and apple notepads. She, of course, has a love-hate relationship with the apples—loves to eat, hates to peel and core. I write this memory up as fall is coming on and apples of every color and variety are showing up in the markets. Apples are so associated with fall, but our tree reaches its production peak in June, so frankly, I associate apples with summer. The tree has slowed down production, but it is still a beautiful tree. My and Daddy's tree.

1   cup vegetable oil

3   eggs

2   cups sugar

2½ cups all-purpose flour

2   teaspoons baking powder

1   teaspoon salt

1   teaspoon baking soda

1   teaspoon ground cinnamon

1   teaspoon ground nutmeg

3   large baking apples, peeled, cored, and finely
    chopped (use a mix of firm apples such as McIntosh,
    Granny Smith, Northern Spy, and Jonagold)

6   ounces butterscotch chips

1 Preheat the oven to 350°F. Spray a 9 by 13-inch baking dish with cooking spray.

2 In the bowl of an electric mixer, thoroughly combine the oil, eggs. and sugar. Sift the flour, baking powder, salt, baking soda, cinnamon, and nutmeg together in a separate bowl, then add to the oil mixture in the mixer, beating until thoroughly combined. The batter will be thick.

3 Use a sturdy spoon to stir in the apple pieces. Scrape the mixture into the prepared pan, spreading it out evenly. Sprinkle the butterscotch chips over the top, lightly pressing them into the batter.

4 Bake for 45 minutes to 1 hour, until golden and pulling away from the sides of the pan slightly.

5 Cool thoroughly and cut into squares.

Bacon Caramels

CYNTHIA FUREY
IRVINE, CALIFORNIA
FUREY & THE FEAST
http://www.fureyandthefeast.com/2009/09/bacon-caramels

I am an editor and freelance food writer living in southern California. I am currently a contributing editor for *Orange Coast* magazine, where I write a monthly feature about what chefs cook when they're at home. I also write "Food 101" for the *Orange County Register*, a column with original recipes that's aimed at helping newbie cooks get over their fear of the kitchen. I am also a Zagat Guide editor and copyeditor for Leite's Culinaria, a James Beard award-winning website. My own website, Furey & the Feast, contains recipes, writings, and food photography.

MAKES 80 TO 100 CARAMELS

Am I too late for this bandwagon? If bacon has left the building and ham is the new swine product of choice, then I'm totally running a little behind on the up-and-up here. It's like I got the memo that bacon was on the out, but I tossed it into a pile of other memos that include not wearing acid-wash jeans after 1986 and how Pluto isn't a planet anymore. Bacon is so last year, the memo says. Artisanal ham is what we're supposed to be doing now. But guys, I dunno about this. The eighties can have its acid wash, but as for bacon and Pluto, I can't let go. Not yet. And bacon! What has it ever done to us to make us want to drop it like a hot potato? This bacon thing, to me, is not a fling. There is still so much to explore before we throw in the towel. Fortunately, there are others that feel the same way about both Pluto and bacon. And, if the meat candy's decline is ultimately imminent, so be it. We tried. But let's send bacon out with a bang, shall we?

14   strips bacon

2   cups sugar

½   cup water

½   cup light corn syrup

1   cup heavy cream

1   cup (2 sticks) butter

2   teaspoons vanilla extract

1 Preheat the oven to 400°F. Line a rimmed baking sheet with parchment paper. Lay the bacon strips on the sheet and bake in the oven for 20 to 25 minutes, or until crispy. Transfer the bacon to a paper towel–lined plate to cool. Crumble 5 to 6 strips of bacon and leave the rest in strips.

2 Line a 9 by 13-inch (or larger!) rimmed baking sheet with parchment. Melt the sugar along with the water and corn syrup in a heavy-bottomed pot over medium-high heat. Let the mixture bubble and stir occasionally to evaporate the water. The sugar will begin to caramelize and turn a lovely shade of amber.

3 Use a thermometer to monitor the caramel. When it reaches 320°F and is golden brown in color, slowly whisk in the cream, butter, and vanilla until completely combined. When the caramel reaches 243°F, remove from the heat and pour into the lined baking sheet. Cool for 15 minutes and add the bacon strips. Cool further, until the caramel is pliable and easier to handle.

4 Invert the pan onto a cutting board so that the bacon strips are on the bottom and the parchment paper is on the top. Remove the parchment paper. Starting at the narrow end, roll the caramel and bacon strips jelly roll style once, and cut creating a log. Continue to roll and cut until you've finished off the pan. Cut the bacon caramel logs into bite-sized pieces. Top with reserved bacon bits.

5 Serve on a platter or roll in wax paper. Keep refrigerated, but let come to room temperature before eating. These will keep for about a week in the refrigerator.

Berry and Ricotta Danishes

There's something magical and fascinating about puff pastry and the way the buttery dough rises up to form anywhere from 513 to 1,459 crisp, golden layers. This week I'll be learning, for a second time, how to make puff pastry from scratch. I first made it at the Pacific Culinary Institute in Vancouver. It was time-consuming work requiring what seemed like endless rolling combined with deft handling of the dough. And then there was the butter. Oh so much of it, carefully and methodically rolled in between layers!

It is thought that early puff pastry found its origins in Rome but was then reintroduced and perfected in the seventeenth century by legendary French chef Marie Antoine Carême. Carême, who likened the art of pastry to architecture, is credited with developing the six-turn method that resulted in unparalleled layers of light, flaky pastry. While I'm not creating the kind of otherworldly delights found in Paris's Poilâne, I am winning friends nonetheless thanks to Carême store-bought pastry. Unlike other ready-made pastry, Carême is actually handmade using natural ingredients. Based in South Australia's Barossa Valley, Carême sells four types of artisan pastry, including sour cream shortcrust and all-butter puff pastry, which I used to make these berry and ricotta Danishes.

SYRIE WONGKAEW
SYDNEY, NEW SOUTH WALES, AUSTRALIA
TASTE BUDDIES
http://allthingsnice.typepad.com/
tastebuddies/2009/11/berry-ricotta-danishes.html

I have been passionate about food my whole life. My real job is in graphic design, but every spare moment is spent in contemplation or concocting of food. Since I bought a good camera, I've been sharing my kitchen creations with the world. I am also the New York Times Company's About.com guide to Australian and New Zealand food.

MAKES 6 DANISHES

PASTRY:

1 sheet store-bought puff pastry

POACHED BERRIES:

12 strawberries, washed, hulled, and halved

½ cup blueberries, washed

2 tablespoons superfine sugar

2 tablespoons water

RICOTTA FILLING:

1 cup ricotta cheese

¼ cup superfine sugar

1 egg yolk

1 teaspoon vanilla extract

½ teaspoon grated lemon zest

2 tablespoons all-purpose flour

GLAZE:

¼ cup confectioners' sugar

3 tablespoons fresh lemon juice

Confectioners' sugar for dusting

1 Thaw the puff pastry according to the package instructions. Once thawed, place the pastry in the fridge to keep it cool while you prepare the other ingredients. Line a baking sheet with parchment paper.

2 Place the strawberries and blueberries in a saucepan over medium-low heat. Sprinkle on the superfine sugar and add the water. Cover the saucepan with a lid and shake the saucepan around to coat the berries. Poach the berries for about 5 minutes, or until they soften but retain their shape. Set aside to cool.

3 Preheat the oven to 350°F.

4 Make the ricotta filling by combining all the ingredients in a mixing bowl. Mix well with a wooden spoon to combine thoroughly.

5 Put the glaze ingredients in a small bowl and mix until smooth. Set aside.

6 Remove the pastry from the refrigerator and place the sheet on a clean, dry surface. Use a small, sharp knife to cut twelve 3¼ inches by 2⅓-inch rectangles. Place 6 of the pastry rectangles on the lined baking sheet, making sure there is space in between them as they will expand. Lightly brush the edges with a little water. We will call these the "pastry rectangle bases."

7 Cut smaller rectangles out of the remaining 6 pastry rectangles so that you have strips of about ½-inch in width. Place the strips on top of the pastry bases, wrapping them around the top edge to create a frame to hold the filling. Fill the middle of the pastry frame with 2 tablespoons of ricotta filling. Top with several berries (reserve some for topping once the Danish are baked). Repeat the process with the remaining pastries.

8 Place in the oven and bake for 15 to 18 minutes, or until the pastry puffs up and is golden. Remove from the oven and cool on a wire rack. Top with the glaze and a little of the remaining poached berries. Sprinkle on a little confectioners' sugar just before serving.

Blueberry Compote Bread Pudding with Soft Curd Cheese Sabayon

The name might be long, but the flavors of this luscious dessert will have you pining for more. More of the blueberries, more of the cinnamon bread pudding, and more of the soft cheese and Cointreau sabayon sauce.

Bake the cinnamon rolls a day ahead of time. Then let them sit out, overnight, so that they harden slightly and get a bit stale. Do not put the icing on the cinnamon rolls. If you do not have the time to make quark (the soft curd cheese), you can substitute ricotta cheese. But I highly recommend that you make the quark. You'll have plenty of it left over, but it can be used within a week as a spread or any way you would normally use ricotta cheese.

PAMELA
LOS ANGELES, CALIFORNIA
MY MAN'S BELLY
http://mymansbelly.com/2009/12/01/blueberry-compote-bread-pudding-with-soft-curd-cheese-sabayon

By day I am a sales and marketing consultant who cooks in between calls, meetings, and other goings-on. By night I am a domestic goddess (LOL).

SERVES 4

SOFT CURD CHEESE (QUARK):

2   quarts buttermilk

BLUEBERRY COMPOTE:

1   12-ounce bag fresh or frozen blueberries

3   tablespoons sugar

1   tablespoon lemon juice

BREAD PUDDING:

2   tablespoons unsalted butter

1   egg

2   tablespoons sugar

¾   cup half-and-half

1   12-ounce can cinnamon rolls, baked, 1 day old, and cut into ½-inch pieces

SABAYON SAUCE:

2   egg yolks

2   tablespoons sugar

2   tablespoons Cointreau

¼   cup soft curd cheese (quark)

1 To make soft curd cheese, preheat the oven to 170°F. Pour the buttermilk into a Dutch oven. Cover and bake for 6 to 8 hours. Line a colander with a double layer of cheesecloth and pour the contents of the Dutch oven into the colander. Drain for 2 hours, then put into a covered container and chill in the refrigerator.

2 To make the blueberry compote, place the blueberries, sugar, and lemon juice in a medium saucepan over medium-high heat. Stir until the ingredients are combined and the blueberries start to break down and release their juices, 15 to 20 minutes. Remove from the heat and set aside.

3 To make the bread pudding, preheat the oven to 350°F. Melt the butter in a microwave and set aside.

4 In a small bowl, whisk the egg, sugar, and half-and-half until thoroughly combined. Once the butter has cooled almost to room temperature, whisk it into the egg mixture. It may appear to curdle a bit . . . don't worry about it. The curds should not be cooked egg; they should be droplets of butter.

5 Divide the blueberry compote among four 8-ounce ramekins. Add cinnamon roll pieces on top of the blueberries. Pour the egg mixture evenly over the tops of the cinnamon roll pieces. Let the ramekins sit for 30 to 60 minutes, occasionally pressing the bread down lightly to help the egg mixture soak into the cinnamon roll pieces. Be careful not to push so hard as to cause the blueberry juices to come to the top.

6 Place the ramekins in the oven and bake for 40 to 45 minutes, until the tops are golden brown and the contents have puffed up.

7 To make the sauce, put the egg yolks, sugar, and Cointreau into the top of a double boiler. Make sure the bottom of the pan does not touch the hot water below or your sauce will curdle. Whisk vigorously until the mixture is light yellow. Whisk in the soft curd cheese and keep whisking until the sauce is light and frothy. Spoon the sauce over the tops of the bread puddings and serve.

Cartellate

You ask what could be more decadent, and I say absolutely nothing. *Cartellate* are traditionally made during Christmas season. They are traditional Pugliese fried pastries filled with roasted almonds, honey, spices, and chocolate. Apulia is a peninsula that forms the heel on the "boot" of Italy. Referred to as a melting pot, it has had many conquerors—Greeks, Romans, Goths, Lombards, Byzantines, Arabs, Normans, Angevins, Aragonese, Spanish, the German emperors, Bourbons, Turks, Venetians, and more—all of whom left their mark on the region. The influences of these cultures are evident in the food and none more than *Cartellate*.

Cartellate is dough mixed with wine, formed into a wagon wheel shape, and fried. The pockets in the wheel are the receptacles for honey or *mosto cotto* (a syrup made from fruits or grape skins), spices, nuts, and chocolate. I have eaten many *cartellate* in Puglia, where the syrup is mostly made with honey or *mosto cotto*, mixed with lemon zest and walnuts. Some have no nuts and might have a scent of cinnamon.

I can honestly say my aunt's recipe is the best. My aunt filled hers with roasted almonds, chocolate, spices, both cinnamon and clove, melted in honey. The combination is positively addicting. In earlier times my family made them only at Thanksgiving and Christmas. As time passed and the love of *cartellate* overtook us, we began to make them the star of our Thanksgiving desserts, and today we also make a separate tray of *cartellate* for weddings. These cookies are a labor of love and not easy to make, but the good news is that you can place the shells in a brown paper bag for a few weeks. I make the filling and store it refrigerated in a glass container so that they are ready to fill and take center stage for our holiday desserts. The only problem is that having them around challenges my willpower.

PATRICIA TURO KLOSTERS
SERNEUS, GRAUBÜNDEN, SWITZERLAND
PIACERE—FOOD & TRAVEL WITHOUT RULES!
http://turosdolci.wordpress.com/2009/11/12/
traditional-holiday-cookie-cartellatecluster-are-filled-
with-honey-nuts-spices

Living in a ski resort in the Swiss Alps and roaming around France, Switzerland, and Italy searching for interesting small restaurants, markets, food, people, and wine is a passion I never get tired of. Born in an American-Italian family who started their life in the United States in the food business is where my journey began. I come from the Boston area, where I have a biscotti business with my sister. My husband and I have a software and translation business and have developed bakers' pricing software. My goal is to use my experience to help hobby bakers move their passion into business opportunities. Buon Appetito!

MAKES 30 COOKIES

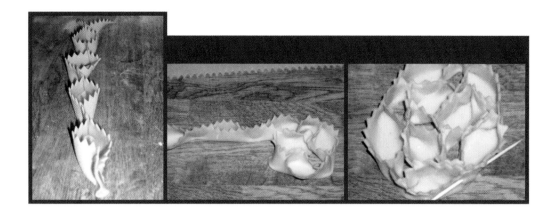

2¾ cups flour

¼ teaspoon sugar

¼ teaspoon salt

¼ cup shortening

1 egg

2¼ teaspoons sherry or Marsala

TO FRY THE PASTRIES:

1 quart canola or peanut oil

FILLING:

24 ounces honey

1 pound roasted almonds, cut in half

1 cup good-quality chopped chocolate
or chocolate chips

1 teaspoon ground cinnamon

1 teaspoon ground cloves

1 Put the flour, sugar, and salt in a bowl or on a board and make a well in the middle. Add the shortening, egg, and sherry. Mix until you can form a ball, adding a little warm water if needed. Knead until the dough is smooth and place it in the refrigerator for about 1 hour, covered with plastic wrap. You can also mix the dough in a food processor.

2 If you have a pasta machine, roll out the dough to its second-to-last level. Or you may roll out a piece with a rolling pin as thinly as possible. Using a pastry cutter with a fluted edge, cut strips about 2 inches wide and 8 inches long.

3 Holding the dough at one end, pinch the dough at intervals about ¾ inch apart, creating small pockets along the strip. Bring the dough around from one end, crimping the dough together and pinching it along the strip to form a circle. These pockets will hold the filling. The cookie looks like a cartwheel, which is the definition of *cartellate*. It should be about 4 inches round; however, they can be made whatever size you want them to be.

4 Secure the ends with a toothpick so that they will not unravel during frying. They will need at least 4 hours of drying time. This is important to keep them from puffing up too much, closing the pockets during frying. You can keep them overnight and fry them the next day.

5 Fry in hot oil about 350°F. Remove when they turn a deep golden color. Allow the shells to dry out on paper towels or on a rack. Remove the toothpicks. If you're not going to fill and eat them right away, place them in a closed paper bag or box until you are ready to fill them.

6 To make the filling, combine all the ingredients in a saucepan and heat over low heat until the chocolate melts. Stir, taste for seasoning, and place in the refrigerator. The filling will get hard but will stay in the shells better if somewhat cool.

7 Start by placing a tablespoon of filling in each cluster cookie. When you have completed this step, go back and keep filling each cookie until you have used all the filling.

8 The filled cookies will keep for a week or more. If you want to make the cookies in advance, place them in a paper bag and they will stay for several days to a month. Never store them in a sealed container or wrap them with plastic wrap.

Chestnut Mousse Mont Blanc

CRISTINA LASARTE
PARIS, FRANCE
CRISTINA, FROM BUENOS AIRES TO PARIS
http://frombatoparis.blogspot.com/2009/12/place-vendome-todays-recipe-chestnut.html

I exchanged English lessons for French pâtisserie and cooking.

MAKES 4 SERVINGS

2 eggs, separated

1 cup mascarpone cheese

1 cup chestnut spread

A few meringue cookies (quantity varies depending on the size of meringue you buy)

WHIPPED CREAM:

1 cup heavy cream

2 teaspoons sugar

4 marrons glacé, a chocolate, or a chocolate truffle

1 In the bowl of a stand mixer, gently whisk the yolks with the mascarpone cheese.

2 Fold in the chestnut spread until combined.

3 In another bowl, whisk the 2 whites to medium stiff peaks. Fold delicately into the mascarpone/chestnut mixture. Refrigerate for 2 to 3 hours.

4 Cut the meringue cookies into small pieces. Put the pieces in four 10-ounce serving glasses.

5 Shortly before serving (otherwise the meringue will absorb the mousse and will "disappear"), pipe or spoon the mousse over the meringue pieces.

6 Make the whipped cream using a mixer (personally I prefer to use an espuma siphon . . . if you use the siphon, prepare this one night in advance). Pipe the sweetened whipped cream on top of the mousse.

7 Place one marron glacé on top of each glass as decoration. If you can't get marrons, use a chocolate or a chocolate truffle.

MARTHA MILLER
ALEXANDRIA, VIRGINIA
A MEASURED MEMORY
http://marthamiller.wordpress.com/2010/02/26/
chocolate-hand-pies

This week's recipe is a take on a childhood favorite, albeit a touch healthier than the version I knew back then. Hand pies are fairly ubiquitous throughout the South and in true southern fashion are almost always fried. I was fortunate to grow up in a household with parents who placed great emphasis on healthy eating. From a very young age we were exposed to and even enjoyed the likes of asparagus, lentil soup, and brown rice. We ate plain Cheerios for breakfast, no sugary Honey Nut, and only on our birthdays tasted the contents of those colorful, cartoon character–fronted boxes that lined the cereal aisles. Strict? Perhaps, but as a result I grew up healthy and with a taste for a wide array of flavors and foods that many of my schoolmates would scrunch up their noses at. Plus, we had a few characters in our life to sneak us a forbidden treat here and there.

Chocolate Hand Pies

In addition to Mrs. Supler and her contraband Kit Kat Bars next door, there was our babysitter Tootie. A quirky lady to be sure, she had a gruffness about her and easily smoked two packs a day. She loved raw onions and would sit at our kitchen table with a knife, peel a layer, eat, repeat. She let us watch trashy daytime soap operas and eat Vienna sausages straight out of the can. And my favorite, she made stacks of Bisquick pancakes sandwiched around a stick of butter and doused in chocolate syrup. Her husband, James, would occasionally drop by for lunch, the imprint of a chewing tobacco canister in the pocket of his workman's trousers. He was the yin to Tootie's yang, with soft eyes and the kind of callused hands that speak to a life of hardness. He always brought something for us. Sometimes a Moon Pie or two, but more often than not, fried chocolate hand pies. I loved the feel of the waxy wrapper and even at a young age knew that this was the most sinful junk food of all. So here I offer my version: baked instead of fried and homemade as opposed to full of artificial sweeteners and trans fat, yet still no model for good health. But if growing up eating my vegetables taught me anything, it's that we all earn a little sin now and again.

MAKES 12 HAND PIES

PASTRY:

2 cups all-purpose flour

½ teaspoon salt

½ cup solid white vegetable shortening, cold and diced

½ cup unsalted butter, cold and diced

1½ teaspoons white vinegar

1 large egg, lightly beaten

PASTRY CREAM:

3¼ cups milk

2 teaspoons plus ½ cup sugar

3 fine strips lemon zest

7 egg yolks

1 whole egg

¼ teaspoon salt

½ cup all-purpose flour

1 tablespoon vanilla extract

3 tablespoons unsalted butter

½ cup cocoa powder, unsweetened
or Dutch process

EGG WASH:

1 egg yolk

1 teaspoon water

CHOCOLATE GLAZE:

1 teaspoon milk

2 teaspoons pastry cream

TOPPING:

½ cup thinly sliced almonds, lightly toasted
Confectioners' sugar

1 To make the pastry, sift the flour and salt into the bowl of a food processor. Pulse lightly to combine. Add the shortening and butter and pulse until it is the size of peas. Add the vinegar, egg, and just enough ice water to moisten, usually 4 to 6 tablespoons. Pulse until the dough just comes together. Wrap dough in plastic and refrigerate at least 30 minutes prior to rolling out.

2 Line 2 or 3 baking sheets with parchment. On a lightly floured surface, roll out the pastry dough until it is ⅛ to ¼ inch thick. Using a small bowl about 4 inches in diameter as a stencil, cut out circles of dough and place on the lined pans.

3 As you fill up each baking sheet, place it in the refrigerator to chill while you gather up the dough scraps, roll out, and cut more circles. If the dough becomes too warm, return it to the refrigerator for 15 minutes to chill. You should have 12 dough circles. Chill for at least 1 hour and up to 1 day.

4 While the dough chills, make the pastry cream. In a double boiler or large heatproof bowl set over a pan of simmering water, heat the milk, 2 teaspoons of the sugar, and the lemon zest just until the mixture comes to a boil.

5 Meanwhile, whisk the remaining ½ cup of sugar, the egg yolks, whole egg, and salt in a small bowl until thick and pale yellow in color, 2 to 3 minutes. Gradually sift in the flour, whisking vigorously to mix. Slowly drizzle ½ cup of the boiling pastry cream into the egg mixture to temper it, then pour the eggs back into the cream.

6 Cook the cream over medium-high heat, whisking frequently, until thickened, 2 to 3 minutes. As the cream thickens and reaches a boil, it may look lumpy. Whisk briskly to smooth. When it reaches the consistency of mayonnaise, reduce the heat and cook for 1 minute more, whisking constantly.

7 Remove from the heat, add the vanilla, and stir in the butter 1 tablespoon at a time. Cool as quickly as possible by placing the bowl in a larger bowl of ice water. Be careful not to let any water leak into the cream.

8 Press plastic wrap over the top to prevent a skin from forming and chill in the refrigerator for at least 1 hour. The pastry cream will keep in the refrigerator for 4 to 5 days or in the freezer for 2 months.

9 Preheat the oven to 350°F. Remove the pastry cream from the refrigerator and bring to room temperature. Whisk in the cocoa until the mixture is smooth.

10 In a small bowl, mix together the egg yolk and water to form the egg wash.

11 To make the chocolate glaze, mix together the milk and the chocolate pastry cream in a small bowl.

12 Remove the dough circles from the fridge, one baking sheet at a time, and place 3 to 4 tablespoons of chocolate pastry cream on one side of each circle, leaving a 1-inch border.

13 With a pastry brush, paint the egg wash on the edges and fold the naked side of the dough over the side with the pastry cream to form a half moon. Crimp with the edges of a fork to seal. Paint the top with the chocolate glaze and sprinkle on the sliced almonds. Repeat with the remaining dough circles.

14 Bake the hand pies for 18 to 22 minutes, until golden. Cool completely on a wire rack and dust with confectioners' sugar. Store the hand pies in an airtight container in the refrigerator for up to 2 days.

SPRINKLEBAKES
KNOXVILLE, TENNESSEE
SPRINKLE BAKES
http://www.sprinklebakes.com/2010/01/chocolate-soup-for-two.html

I have always been fond of that sweet, usually last course of a meal, but I wasn't always a baker and dessert maker. For years, I was an aspiring painter. I still paint, but I have found a new joy in the art of baking and sugar craft. I try my best to assemble delightful desserts that are as artful as they are delicious.

SERVES 2

Chocolate Soup for Two

Valentine's Day is exactly one month away, and I'm elbow-deep in chocolate recipes. I've been searching for ideas and inspiration for sweet, edible tokens of affection. Recently, while watching a food show on TV, I saw chocolate soup being served at a popular chocolate bar/buffet. Patrons were proclaiming their love (between slurps of soup) for the warm, velvety smoothness and rich chocolaty flavor. I got out a pen and paper and wrote, "find chocolate soup." In my search I've found so many variations on chocolate soup, I didn't know which one to try. They all sounded so rich and almost too heavy. Does anyone really want a heavy dessert on date night? After a few trial runs, I decided to make my own.

I wanted to lighten the soup without compromising the richness or velvety texture. I mixed skim milk with fat-free half-and-half to maintain the creamy texture. I also found that I could not tell the difference (in the completed soup) between the fat-free and regular sweetened condensed milk. One of my favorite elements of this dish is the marshmallow and cream cheese garnish. It provides an interesting and needed flavor contrast.

The variations on this recipe are as numerous as there are varieties of chocolate. I imagine an orange-infused chocolate bar would pair well with a little Grand Marnier in this soup. A big fat biscotti crouton (or many of them) would be a delicious addition. This dessert should be served warm. It's rich and velvety, just like the full-fat version, like a rich chocolate pudding. I have a jar of gourmet ice cream topping called "chocolate crunch" that I used for further garnishing.

Chocolate Soup would be an excellent Valentine's Day dessert to share with someone special, even if that someone special is your grandma. I view the holiday as a celebration of all kinds of love, and not just the romantic variety.

1 cup skim milk

1 cup fat-free half-and-half

⅓ cup fat-free sweetened condensed milk

1 teaspoon vanilla extract

1 cup bittersweet chocolate chips or
   1 six-ounce bar of chocolate, chopped

2 tablespoons cornstarch

2 tablespoons cold water

2 ounces low-fat cream cheese, for garnish

2 tablespoons heaping marshmallow crème, for garnish

1 In a medium saucepan over medium heat, stir together the skim milk, half-and-half, sweetened condensed milk, and vanilla extract. Bring almost to a boil. Reduce the heat to low, add the chocolate, and whisk until the chocolate melts. In a separate small bowl, combine the cornstarch and water to form a slurry. Add the slurry a little at a time to the chocolate mixture, whisking constantly, until the soup is thick and smooth. You will know it is ready when the bubbles are gone and the chocolate has thickened, 5 to 7 minutes. Carefully pour into 2 bowls.

2 Microwave the cream cheese in a microwave-safe container at 10-second intervals, or until it can be stirred smooth. Add the marshmallow crème to the cream cheese and mix well. Dollop on top of the soup or transfer the cream to a pastry bag and pipe a design on top of each bowl.

Cranberry Crumb Bars

Just how good are these Cranberry Crumb Bars? As Mary Poppins would say, they're practically perfect in every way. I have made 3 pans of them just this week. Practically perfect, see? Verging on actual perfection minus the part about how they aren't exactly health food.

Okay, before you go all "Oh my gosh are you crazy?" and "That's so bad for you" on me, let me justify those three pans first. Okay? Pan number 1: We devoured them. I had the last one for breakfast yesterday because it was calling my name in the fridge. The pan was just taking up way too much space since it wasn't really serving any purpose by housing only one bar. Pans number 2 and 3: Logan and Madeline had a grand time helping me press the crust in and then littered the kitchen with flour, sugar, and baking powder. I was also trying to make Beef with Broccoli for dinner at the same time. Am I crazy or what? Please don't answer that. Pan number 2 is for Moms Club Garage Sale/Bake Sale tomorrow morning. Pan number 3 part 1 is for a friend's family. Pan number 3 part two is for us. Again. I could hardly wait for them to chill before (a) delivering them and (b) eating them myself. So I ate some unchilled, and they were a mess to cut into, but still really good. I also think they're the perfect treat for the upcoming holidays or any time you want your kitchen to smell awesome. P.S. Cranberries are good for you. Right? Right.

KATIE GOODMAN
ALBUQUERQUE, NEW MEXICO
GOODLIFE {EATS}
http://www.goodlifeeats.com/2009/10/cranberry-crumb-bars.html

Part of the goodness in life is sharing good food with friends and family. I'm a stay-at-home mom (now a part-time work-at-home mom) determined to make family meal time a priority while providing a variety of healthy and delicious food choices. On my blog, I share what I find good in the kitchen and in life. I also work as a freelance food contributor to Paula Deen Online and Craftzine.

MAKES ABOUT 24 BARS

DOUGH:

1 cup sugar

2½ cups all-purpose flour

½ cup almond meal

¼ teaspoon salt

1 teaspoon baking powder

1 cup (2 sticks) cold butter

1 egg

CRANBERRY FILLING:

⅔ cup sugar

1 tablespoon cornstarch

1 teaspoon vanilla extract

Juice of ½ orange

4 cups fresh cranberries

¼ teaspoon ground cinnamon

1 Preheat the oven to 375°F. Butter a 9 by 13-inch pan.

2 To make the crust, mix together the sugar, flour, almond meal, salt, and baking powder in a medium bowl. Use a fork or pastry cutter to blend in the butter and egg. The dough will be crumbly. Alternatively, pulse the dry ingredients in a food processor with the butter until the dough is pebbly and then mix in the egg until it all comes together. Pat half of the dough into the buttered pan.

3 To make the filling, stir together the sugar, cornstarch, vanilla, and orange juice in another bowl. Mix in the cranberries. Sprinkle the cranberry mixture evenly over the dough in the pan.

4 Add the cinnamon to the remaining dough, then crumble the dough over the berries. Bake for 45 to 55 minutes, or until the top is a light golden brown. Cool completely and chill in the refrigerator before cutting into squares. Store in an airtight container in the refrigerator for up to 3 days.

NOTE: If you can't find almond meal, toss almonds in a food processor until finely ground.

Favorite Moist Chocolate Cake

CHERI
OSLO, NORWAY
KITCHEN SIMPLICITY
http://kitchensimplicity.com/moist-chocolate-cake/

With a love of cooking, baking, decorating, and serving, I am a self-taught culinary blogger. A wife, mother, and Canadian expat, I live in the land of fjords. I fell in love with cooking in college, but it wasn't until recently that I began sharing my love of food and explorations of new recipes on KitchenSimplicity.com. My simple approach to food is to inspire and teach others to cook more simply without sacrifice of quality or flare.

SERVES 12

When I was in high school, my sister-in-law and I decided to make a cake as a surprise for my mom's birthday. We successfully snuck her trusty mixer out of the house to the church next door, giddy with excitement that we were going to pull off such a wonderful surprise. We got to work, with me manning the mixer and feeling ultra-important. I was doing so well and everything was going swimmingly. I left the mixer for a moment and continued on my merry way to complete the other important tasks in front of me. Suddenly we were startled by a grinding, gargling sound as the mixer gasped for air. We rushed to its aid and discovered that I had left the spatula in the bowl and it had gotten tangled in the beaters. We tried to free it from its agonizing pain, but it was too late. The motor had burnt out. It had died a painful and tragic death. We hung our heads and carried the lifeless mixer back to the house. Happy Birthday, Mom! Surprise?

Thankfully I have an understanding mom who likes to laugh in the face of adversity (in this case probably to keep from crying). Since then I have become a much better cook and hopefully a little wiser. I have made many a cake with no one's mixer being the worse for it. Including this one. I actually like to mix this cake by hand because it is so easy to whip up and dirties only one bowl. I have made this cake on numerous occasions, and it is a definite favourite. It is chocolaty, moist, and delicious. It goes with many fillings and variations. I made this cake for my son's first birthday back in June. I froze it, along with its filling of Strawberry Cheesecake Mousse, and topped it with ganache, which made for an icy delight. But this is one cake that I can eat completely on its own with no icings or fillings. Not too sweet and just perfect.

CHOCOLATE CAKE:

2 cups all-purpose flour

1 teaspoon salt

1 teaspoon baking powder

2 teaspoons baking soda

¾ cup baking cocoa

2 cups sugar

1 cup vegetable oil

1 cup brewed coffee

1 cup milk

2 eggs

1 teaspoon vanilla extract

STRAWBERRY CHEESECAKE MOUSSE:

4 ounces cream cheese

¼ cup sugar

½ cup puréed strawberries

¾ cup cold heavy cream

GANACHE:

1 cup heavy cream

9 ounces bittersweet chocolate, chopped

Fresh strawberries, for garnish

1 To make the cake, preheat the oven to 325°F. Grease and flour two 9-inch round pans.

2 Sift together the flour, salt, baking powder, baking soda, cocoa, and sugar into a large bowl. Add the oil, coffee, and milk. Whisk until combined. Add the eggs and vanilla. Whisk until well incorporated, about 2 minutes. The batter will be quite runny.

3 Pour the batter into the pans and bake for 25 to 30 minutes, until a toothpick inserted into the centre comes out clean. Let the cakes cool in the pans for 10 minutes before removing to cool completely.

4 To make the mousse, mix the cream cheese and sugar in a bowl until completely smooth. Stir in the puréed strawberries. Whip the cream to stiff peaks in another bowl and fold into the strawberry cream cheese.

5 Line a 9-inch round pan (the same size you used for the cakes) with plastic wrap and pour in the mousse. Freeze until solid.

6 To make the ganache, bring the cream to a boil over medium heat in a small saucepan. Pour it over the chocolate. Let sit for a moment, then stir until smooth. Cool to room temperature.

7 To assemble the cake, remove the mousse from the freezer and unwrap it. Place one cake layer on a serving platter. Position the frozen mousse on top and top with the remaining cake layer. Allow to thaw for 30 minutes or so.

8 Drizzle with ganache and garnish with fresh strawberries.

Gluten-Free Quinoa and Corn Flour Crêpes with Strawberry-Maple Filling

NIKKI GARDNER
WILLIAMSBURG, MASSACHUSETTS
ART AND LEMONS
http://www.artandlemons.com/2009/07/playlist-for-crepes-part-one.html

When I was younger, I hated lemons unless they were coated with spoonfuls of sugar. Even sugar could not bring me to love this tart citrus. Until, one day, years later, the inevitable happened. I bit into my first lemon curd bar, turning distaste into obsession.

MAKES ABOUT 12 CRÊPES, SERVING 6

Lately the nights are soaked in rain and thunderclaps. I dream about jazz and crêpes. When I wake up, I remember songs from Woody Allen's film *Stardust Memories* and decide to make crêpes. The setup: If you're making morning or midday crêpes, brew a cup of tea or coffee to sip as you cook. For evening or dessert crêpes, pour a glass of wine, a white or red burgundy—either way you can't go wrong—and taste. Included is my suggested play list for making crêpes.

1. "Begin the Beguine" by Artie Shaw and His Orchestra. Gather ingredients: One 8- to 10-inch nonstick skillet. Quinoa, corn, and tapioca flours. Xanthan gum. Sea salt. Hemp milk. Flaxseeds. Coconut oil. Maple syrup. Time for warm-up exercises.

2. "Flight of the Bumblebee" by Harry James and His Orchestra. Prepare to sweat a bit. Crêpes take some practice to master the art of flipping. Put on your matching wrist and head bands. Jog in place, up to 2 minutes. Warm up your wrists for crêpe flipping by doing wrist rotations (both hands), 20 rotations left and right. Finish with 10 jumping jacks. Now you're ready to make the crêpe batter.

3. "Stardust" by Louis Armstrong and His Orchestra. Hydrate with a glass of water. Grind the flaxseeds. Melt the coconut oil. Mix separately, dry and wet ingredients. Combine. Add more hemp milk for a pourable batter. Take a sip of your beverage of choice.

4. "I'll See You in My Dreams" by Django Reinhardt. Heat the nonstick skillet. Pour batter into the pan with one hand as you swirl the pan in the other to coat the batter. Accept that your first and second crêpes will be failures and clump together like fluffy cumulus clouds. Remember: You are not alone. After the first two tries, your crêpes will be flat as flat and round as LP records.

5. "Did I Remember (To Tell You I Adore You)" by Billie Holiday and Her Orchestra, Bunny Berigan, Artie Shaw. Bask in the glory of success. Pour more batter. Repeat flipping technique. Store cooked crêpes in the oven on low heat. Serve with sweet or savory fillings.

6. "Goodbye" by Benny Goodman. Wrap unused crêpes in foil and refrigerate. When ready to eat, reheat in a 325°F. oven. As the sun sifts through the curtains only to be overshadowed minutes later by another downpour of rain, sit down with a crêpe sprinkled with maple sugar and fresh lemon juice. Enjoy your crêpe success while you watch *Stardust Memories*—you've earned a break.

CRÊPES:

½ cup quinoa flour

½ cup corn flour (different from cornmeal)

⅓ cup tapioca flour

½ teaspoon xanthan gum

¼ teaspoon sea salt

2½ to 3 cups hemp milk (or use soy, almond, or rice milk)

1 tablespoon ground flaxseeds whisked
   with 3 tablespoons boiling water

1 tablespoon pure maple syrup

2 tablespoons virgin coconut oil,
   melted, plus more for the pan

FILLING:

½ teaspoon coconut oil

5 cups ripe strawberries

2 tablespoons pure maple syrup

   Dash of rum (optional)

1 Whisk the flours, xanthan gum, and salt together in a bowl. In a separate bowl, whisk 2½ cups of the hemp milk, the flaxseed mixture, maple syrup, and the melted coconut oil together. Add the wet ingredients to the dry ingredients and gently mix together. If the batter is too thick, add a few tablespoons of hemp milk at a time, up to ½ cup more hemp milk to make a pourable batter. (The batter should be thin enough to spread easily in the pan.) Allow the batter to rest in the refrigerator for at least 30 minutes.

2 In the meantime, prepare the filling. Heat the coconut oil in a medium saucepan over medium heat. Cook the strawberries, maple syrup, and rum until a jammy syrup forms. Remove from the heat and add more syrup and rum to taste. Set aside.

3 Heat an 8- or 10-inch nonstick skillet over medium heat. Add a small dab of virgin coconut oil for cooking. Pour about ½ cup batter into the skillet and, at the same time, rotate the pan so the batter makes a thin layer on the bottom. Use small amounts of batter to repair any holes; work quickly and keep the crêpe thin. Cook until the top of the is dry. After about 1 minute, loosen the edges of the crêpe from the pan with a spatula. Flip with your fingers or gently toss and flip (this may take a few attempts but works best) and cook the other side for 30 to 60 seconds. Stack the cooked crêpes on a plate. Keep them warm in a low oven or fill each crêpe while it's in the pan. Repeat the process, adding more coconut oil between crêpes as needed, until all the batter is used up.

4 Fill each crêpe with a few tablespoons of filling, roll, and serve. Store any leftover crêpes in the refrigerator wrapped in plastic.

Green Tea–Chocolate Steamed Cupcakes

Steamed cakes are very popular among Asians, and there are various ways to make them. This technique may originate from the time when an oven was not readily available in Asian countries, but a steamer was always available and a cheaper alternative. The Chinese had been making sweet and savory cakes by using a steamer, and the technique spread to various Asian countries. Indonesians also make steamed cupcakes, called *bolu kukus*, using various ingredients like coconut milk or flavored sodas for flavor or pandan leaf juice for color and flavor.

After looking at my friend's picture of steamed cakes, I decided last Sunday was the time to make them. I decided to try combining green tea and cocoa powder, a popular choice nowadays. The cakes turned out very good indeed. Now, the success of steamed cupcakes is measured by how big the cakes will puff up. They have to bloom like flowers from the hot steam to produce what Indonesians calls successful steamed cupcakes. The first time I opened my steamer lid, they puffed very big. I was afraid that they had bloomed too much. But once they cooled down, the puffiness came down a bit and they were perfect. May the bloom force be with you!

ELIZA ADAM
WEST LINN, OREGON
NOTES FROM MY FOOD DIARY
http://fooddiary.blogsome.com/2009/11/03/green-tea-chocolate-steamed-cupcakes

I'm a Chinese-Indonesian who's been living in the Pacific Northwest since 1995. My passion is baking, whether Western or Asian style, but I also cook regularly. Anything I make is about comfort and familiarity, yet I love to try anything new. Developing good taste requires bravery.

MAKES 9 INDIVIDUAL CUPCAKES

1   cup all-purpose flour

½   teaspoon baking powder

1   cup sugar

2   large eggs

5   ounces coconut milk

1   tablespoon green tea powder

2   tablespoons unsweetened cocoa powder

1 Sift together the flour and baking powder into a medium bowl.

2 Prepare individual *bolu kukus* cups, or you can use small individual brioche cups lined with parchment paper, about 2 inches high.

3 With an electric mixer, beat together the sugar and eggs until the batter is ribbony and very pale in color, about 5 to 7 minutes. Alternately add the sifted dry ingredients and the coconut milk, stirring well after each addition.

4 Divide the batter into 2 batches. Using a rubber spatula, mix one-third of the batter with the green tea powder and two-thirds with the cocoa powder until well combined.

5 Prepare a steamer, filling it with water. Have ready a towel to cover the inside of the steamer lid. Heat the steamer over high heat until the water boils very rapidly. Reduce to medium heat while you fill the cups with batters.

6 Using a big ice cream scooper, fill the cups with cocoa batter about three-quarters full. Using a small ice cream scooper or a tablespoon, add the green tea batter on top of the chocolate batter. Tap the cup to the surface to let the batter settle. Repeat with the remaining cups.

7 Place all the cups inside the steamer. Place a towel over the top of the steamer and close the lid carefully. Increase the heat again to high and, once the water returns to a boil, set the timer for 10 minutes. Carefully open the lid and remove the towel. Make sure water drops don't contact the cakes.

8 Turn off the heat and remove the cups. Cool the cakes on a wire rack.

Coconut Israeli Couscous Studded with Pomegranate

Pomegranates are such a magical fruit. Smooth and conservative on the outside, split open, they hit your eye with a lurid flood of color. Intricate rows of delicate seeds sit encased in a honeycomb-like membrane. It takes a little work, but once you are able to persuade the little jewels out, you will be handsomely rewarded with bursts of sweet-tart, antioxidant-richness.

I wondered what I could put together from my pantry to make something tasty with my prize. I had some leftover coconut milk in the fridge, and those big round beads of Israeli couscous in the cupboard caught my eye. The coconut flavor called out for some equally sensuous, exotic, warm spices, like cardamom and a touch of cinnamon. After I cooked the couscous, I studded it with a handful of pomegranate seeds. The juicy pop from them gave a lovely little zing to each comforting bite. I could eat this for breakfast, midafternoon snack, or even dessert. And it took all of maybe 15 minutes to make.

STEPHANIE IM
SAN FRANCISCO, CALIFORNIA
LICK MY SPOON
http://lickmyspoon.com/recipes/pomegranates

I'm a food writer and flavor chaser.

SERVES 4

8   pods green cardamom

1   cup milk

1   cup coconut milk (I prefer unsweetened so I can control the amount of sugar)

1   cup Israeli couscous

¼   teaspoon ground cinnamon

1   tablespoon sugar

½   cup pomegranate seeds

1   Smash the cardamom pods open with the flat side of your knife (like a garlic clove).

2   Combine the milk, coconut milk, and cardamom in a sauce-pan and place over low heat. Bring to just below a boil, stirring every once in a while. It will be a little foamy. Strain the cardamom pods out since the shells are not so good to eat.

3   Add the couscous and simmer over low heat for 10 to 12 minutes, until all the liquid is absorbed. The couscous should be tender but with some chew to it.

4   Stir in the cinnamon, sugar, and pomegranate seeds.

VARIATION: If you don't have pomegranate seeds, or don't like them, try substituting raisins or dried cranberries.

Lime S'More Tartlets

ULTERIOR EPICURE
KANSAS CITY, MISSOURI
THE ULTERIOR EPICURE
http://ulteriorepicure.com/2007/09/12/campfire-in-the-keys

I am an anonymous blogger. I live to travel and eat.

MAKES SIX 4½-INCH TARTLETS

In Kansas City, where I grew up, they used to have Tippins restaurants–cum–pie counters at various locations around the city (think Marie Callender's for those of you on the West Coast or Baker's Square for northern Midwesterners). Conveniently, one happened to be on the way back home from church. There was a good stretch of time when my family would stop in, without fail, after service to pick up a pie (or two) for the week.

Everyone had their favorite, and to mitigate fighting among siblings, my parents rotated between my siblings for each week's pick. Even as a child, I was not a goopy saccharin eater, especially not with dessert. Honestly, none of their pies attracted me. I liked the crusts, but otherwise the fillings were too creamy, sweet, and rich. Also, I was allergic to chocolate, so the only pie that really tempted me, the French Silk (think chocolate pudding under layers of whipped cream and shaved dark chocolate), I couldn't have.

When it came time for me to pick, I would always choose lemon meringue (that is, if it wasn't October or November, when pumpkin pie was the must-have). Tart, smooth, and light tasting, it seemed like a palatable alternative to the others. But to be honest, it wasn't the curd that I really liked; it was the airy, fluffy, and wonderful cloud of toasted meringue, piled sky-high, on top that got me. It was *magical.* How did they do that? It was better than marshmallow. It wasn't sweet, and it didn't stick to my teeth.

Sadly, over the years, Tippins restaurants closed across town. Today, the company is still going strong, but selling its pies only through local grocery stores. Now, in my adulthood, my sweet tooth has grown a bit (no doubt thanks to outgrowing my chocolate allergy) and I've come to appreciate lemon and lime curds. And the magic of meringue stays with me.

Recently, I made a lime tartlet recipe in *Simple Pleasures* by esteemed New York chef Alfred Portale. It inspired me to have a little fun and make one that expresses my personal tastes. This recipe was inspired by a combination of recipes. It will take time and patience. However, given the right tools, it is worth the trouble.

GRAHAM CRUST:

3   packages graham crackers (approximately 24 crackers), roughly broken up

½   teaspoon salt

1¼ cups (2½ sticks) unsalted butter, melted, plus butter for greasing the tart pans

LIME CURD:

¾   cup freshly squeezed lime juice (from 16 to 18 limes)

¾   cup sugar

6   eggs

6   egg yolks

6   ounces (1½ sticks) unsalted butter at room temperature, cut into 12 pieces

      Grated zest of 2 limes

CHOCOLATE GANACHE:

10 ounces bittersweet chocolate (65% recommended), chopped

⅔   cup sugar

7   tablespoons unsalted butter, cut into 7 pieces

MERINGUE:

4   egg whites at room temperature

1   cup sugar

1   teaspoon cream of tartar

1   To prepare the graham crust, preheat the oven to 350°F. Butter six 4½-inch tart pans, preferably springform.

2   Put the graham crackers into a food processor and pulse until the crackers break down to the consistency of sand. Transfer to a large bowl. Stir in the salt and 1¼ cups melted butter and mix until the butter is thoroughly incorporated. The mixture should have the consistency of wet sand.

3   Press and pack the wet graham mixture into the tart pans, making sure the crust goes up all the way on the sides and is thick and sturdy.

4   Arrange the tarts on 1 or 2 cookie sheets and bake for 12 minutes, or until the crusts are golden but not browned. Remove the tart shells from the oven and set aside to cool. The tart crusts can be stored in airtight plastic containers, in a single layer, for up to 24 hours.

5   To prepare the lime curd, put the lime juice, sugar, eggs, and egg yolks in a stainless-steel bowl and whisk well.

6   Half-fill a saucepan with water, bring the water to a boil over high heat, then lower the heat so the water is simmering. Set the bowl over the pot and whisk the lime curd occasionally until it thickens, approximately 10 minutes. Then whisk in the butter, 1 piece at a time. When all of the butter is melted and incorporated, stir in the lime zest and remove the saucepan from the heat. Remove the bowl from the saucepan and let it cool for 5 minutes.

7   Transfer the lime curd to a blender or food processor and blend until very smooth. (I find that using a blender/food processor can be messy and dangerous. I encourage you to use an immersion/hand blender instead if you have one). The curd can be made, cooled, covered, and refrigerated for up to 1 week.

8 Divide the lime curd among the tart shells, filling them about half full. Chill in the refrigerator while making the chocolate ganache or until set.

9 To prepare the chocolate ganache, melt the chocolate together with the sugar and butter in the top of a double boiler (simmer water over low heat in a saucepan and put a heat-resistant bowl on top). Stir constantly until the sugar is well incorporated and the mixture is smooth and shiny. Remove the melted chocolate from the heat and let it cool for 5 minutes.

10 Carefully pour the liquid chocolate ganache over each tartlet, making sure the chocolate does not overflow the graham crust sides. Return the tarts to the refrigerator and chill for 1 to 2 hours, or until the ganache has set. (The ganache should take on a smooth matte finish.)

11 To prepare the meringue and finish the tarts, whip the egg whites in the bowl of a stand mixer fitted with a whip attachment until frothy. Slowly add the sugar, then the cream of tartar, continuing to whip until well incorporated. Increase the stand mixer to medium speed and whip until the whites are shiny and form stiff peaks. Do not overwhip or they will become grainy. Transfer the meringue to a pastry bag fitted with a star tip and pipe it around the edge of each tart. Or transfer it to a large freezer bag, seal tightly, and snip off one corner. Pipe the meringue on as desired.

12 Using a kitchen torch, quickly brown the meringue, being careful not to melt the chocolate ganache on top. (Due to the chocolate ganache layer, the meringues should not be browned under a broiler.) Serve immediately.

Lonely for London Cookies

My favorite city in the world is London. It reminds me of New York, but with an infinitely cleaner and more comfortable subway. London is damp and cool, and, dictated by my Western European genes, is the kind of weather I favor. I was fifteen when I went to London for the first time. My younger brother, Robbie, and I were meeting my dad, who was working in Saudi Arabia, for a few weeks of R&R.

I know London has climbed out of the basement as far as cuisine goes, but when I was there in 1978 the food was pretty bad. Robbie and I subsisted on prawns, fish and chips, and sweet, creamy tea and scones. Even good bread was hard to come by. Robbie and I made an amazing culinary discovery that sustained us through the hard times: Cadbury Whole Nut bars, made with creamy milk chocolate and whole hazelnuts. I had never had a hazelnut before that, and I was hooked. These didn't come in the same 1½-ounce size as our paltry American Hershey bars. These suckers were twice the size of our candy bars back home, and we ate them in their entirety. That summer, I think Robbie and I ate our weights in Whole Nutters, as my dad called them. Whenever I think back to that trip, Robbie's eleven-year-old face is never free of chocolate smears. When I returned home to New York, I was stricken to discover the Whole Nut bar was nowhere to be found. When I went back to England again four years later, I stocked up. I was able to coax various friends and family members into bringing them back for me when they hopped across the pond, but I wasn't getting them with nearly enough regularity.

I conceived these cookies one day when I was missing London and really wanted a Whole Nutter. I sent my chocolate-loving mom a few dozen of these cookies last year for Mother's Day, and I am happy to report she enjoyed them immensely. I think this gesture may have eased some of the pain I caused her as a child by always refusing to eat what she put in front of me.

LORI JABLONS
LOS ANGELES, CALIFORNIA
STUFF TO EAT
http://stuff2eat.blogspot.com/2009/05/london.html

I am a picky eater (however, not a completely phobic, insane one) and transplanted New Yorker who lives in Los Angeles. I'm a magazine editor and writer who loves cooking and baking. My *Playboy* centerfold profile reads: "Lori is a Leo, loves the New York Yankees, landscape photography, puppies, and Wise barbecue potato chips." I've been married to the same guy for twenty-three years, and we have a hilarious teenage son who often jokes his way out of trouble and two dogs who pretty much do the same. Though I'm right-handed, I am trying to train my left hand to be more useful. I'm doing this with my hair as well, but, I have to say, my left hand is making far more progress than my hair.

3 DOZEN COOKIES

There are still days when I miss London intensely, and I am hoping to get back there this summer. I have already cleaned out the suitcase that I will bring to transport my Whole Nutters back home.

½   cup hazelnuts

2   cups all-purpose flour

1   teaspoon baking soda

½   teaspoon salt

1   tablespoon instant espresso powder

½   cup good-quality unsweetened cocoa powder, sifted

1   cup (2 sticks) unsalted butter, melted

¾   cup granulated sugar

¾   cup brown sugar, packed

2   teaspoons vanilla extract

⅓   cup unsweetened all-natural applesauce

⅓   cup unsweetened shredded coconut

1   cup bittersweet chocolate chips (I like Ghirardelli)

1   Preheat the oven to 375°F.

2   Place the hazelnuts on a baking sheet and toast until you can smell them, 8 to 10 minutes. Let cool, then remove the brown papery skins by rubbing the nuts in your hands or a dish towel. It's kind of messy, so I usually do this over the sink. You need to get rid of the skins. They don't taste good. Coarsely chop the nuts and set aside.

3   In a medium bowl, whisk together flour, baking soda, salt, espresso powder, and cocoa powder.

4   In a large bowl, whisk together the melted butter, granulated sugar, brown sugar, and vanilla. Whisk in the applesauce until combined.

5   Add the dry ingredients to the wet ingredients and stir together until combined. Stir in the coconut, chocolate chips, and hazelnuts.

6   Place a piece of parchment paper on an ungreased baking sheet. If you don't want to use parchment, no worries; just don't grease the baking sheet. Drop teaspoonfuls of dough onto the baking sheet. These spread out, so make sure you leave enough room on the baking sheet. Bake for 9 minutes.

7   When you remove the baking sheet from the oven, bang it against the counter to "deflate" the cookies. I usually just drop it kind of hard, and that does the trick. Let cool on the baking sheet for 5 minutes, then transfer to a rack to cool completely.

8   When completely cool, transfer to an airtight container, where they'll keep for about 3 days.

Mango Avocado Ice Cream

In Vietnam, we eat avocados like fruits. Slice one open and sprinkle some sugar on top and just eat it with a spoon. Or whiz together in the blender some avocado, condensed milk, and ice and you've got a hefty smoothie. The first time I saw slices of avocado in a salad, I actually thought it was gross.

Imagine my surprise when a few days ago a close family friend brought us a full box of ripe avocado. A WHOLE BOX! I mean, I've never had more than four avocados at a time in the house. So I went to sleep thinking of all the things I could do with them. I then woke up thinking of them. It was like that for a few days, really obsessive, so I knew I had to make something before my brain exploded green goo. I used to blend avocado and Ataulfo mango together with a touch of lime and eat it chilled like a puddingish dessert. So I thought I could make an ice cream version. And since avocado is already fatty and creamy enough, I went with whole milk instead of cream.

**TRAMIE, MONTREAL
QUEBEC, CANADA
TRAMIE'S KITCHEN**
http://bakingatmidnight.blogspot.com/2009/06/
mango-avocado-ice-cream.html

I love to cook, bake, and most of all, to watch those I love enjoy my creations. I subconsciously refer everything to food. I secretly wish that I could save the world with every cookie that I bake and share with people.

SERVES 8

Flesh of 1 Ataulfo mango

Flesh of 2 ripe avocados

Juice of 1 lime

1 to 1½ cups whole milk

3   tablespoons honey

1 Blend everything together in a blender until smooth.

2 Refrigerate, covered, overnight.

3 Churn in your ice cream maker according to the manufacturer's instructions. Store in the freezer.

Maple Cinnamon Pecan Ice Cream

For years I've had a love and hate thing going for the fall season. I loved the fall because of the cool crisp air, beautiful colors, apples, pumpkins, and all the yummy fall recipes that can be enjoyed only during this time of year. But I hated the fall because of the winter that often comes knocking before I am ready to say good-bye. This year has been very different with living in Costa Rica. We are actually finishing up our winter (rainy season), and the summer (dry season) will start up around December.

So, today I have a great fall ice cream to share with you. The wonderful combination of pecans, maple syrup, and cinnamon really hits the sweet spot. We have actually decided that this ice cream has become the favorite now, but due to limited supply of maple syrup, we can enjoy this only once every few months (when someone—usually my in-laws—comes down to visit and brings a bottle of maple syrup). Yes, we did find a tiny bottle of maple syrup for about $18 at a gringo grocery store, but no way we are spending that much for it.

Back to the ice cream, it is simply delicious and so comforting. Did you know that cinnamon is a great source of manganese, fiber, iron, and calcium? I didn't! I also learned that cinnamon can help lower LDL cholesterol, regulate blood sugar, stop yeast infections, fight E. coli bacteria, reduce arthritis pain, and much more! No wonder it makes me feel so good when I sprinkle some on my toast with raw honey. Adding cinnamon to maple syrup and pecans, with a pinch of sea salt, really made it perfect. If you don't have soaked and dehydrated pecans, use the regular kind, but you will be missing out on some seriously good flavor!

MARILLYN BEARD
COSTA RICA
JUST MAKING NOISE: SOUND BITES FROM A DEAF MAMA
http://just-making-noise.blogspot.com/2009/10/sweet-wholesome-wednesday-maple.html

MAKES ABOUT 2 QUARTS

3   cups whole milk or cream

½   cup maple syrup

3   egg yolks, beaten lightly

1   tablespoon arrowroot powder

1   tablespoon vanilla extract

1   tablespoon ground cinnamon

¾   cup pecans, soaked, dehydrated (or roasted pecans), and chopped

Pinch of sea salt

1   Put all the ingredients in a bowl and mix well. Pour into your ice cream maker and proceed according to the manufacturer's instructions.

2   If you do not have an ice cream maker, simply pour into a plastic sealed container and put in your freezer. When completely frozen, chop it up and put in your blender. Blend until creamy.

KRIS ALCANTARA
RIVER EDGE, NEW JERSEY
MARRIED TO CHOCOLATE
http://www.married2chocolate.com/2009/11/no-bake-mondays-frozen-smores-bars.html

I am a twenty-something food writer living ten miles from Manhattan. Despite being a bridge-and-tunnel girl with no sense of direction, I find my way around New York City by its gourmet chocolate shops. My devotion to dessert gave birth to Married to Chocolate in 2009, while I was completing an MA in magazine and online journalism at Syracuse University. Now a penniless journalist with no lucrative job, I spend my Sundays making no-bake treats and giving them away. I also dabble in photography from time to time and think chocolates make sexy subjects. Rowrrrr.

MAKES 12 BARS

No-Bake Frozen S'Mores Bars

Introducing . . . the most pimped-out s'mores bar ever. This bad boy is made with vanilla yogurt, chocolate-covered grahams, marshmallows, walnuts, heavy cream, and loads of chocolate chips. It's your sweet tooth's dream come true (and possibly your diet's nightmare). Note: vanilla yogurt is optional but adds a nice bite to the bar, like a tangy kick almost as an afterthought, and lets the chocolate go down easy.

½ cup heavy whipping cream

1¼ cups chocolate chips, plus more for garnish

2 cups miniature marshmallows

12 pieces chocolate-covered graham crackers, broken into bite-size pieces

2 cups vanilla yogurt

Walnuts for garnish

Graham cracker crumbs (about 3 crackers) for garnish

1 Heat the whipping cream in a saucepan for 2 minutes, or until the edges start to bubble.

2 Remove from the heat. Add chocolate chips and stir until smooth. Wait about 10 minutes, then add the marshmallows and graham cracker pieces. Stir to combine, then add the vanilla yogurt and mix well.

3 Line a baking pan (or whatever container you want) with foil. Spread the batter in the pan. Top with walnuts and more chocolate chips. Chill for at least 2 hours, then cut into bars.

Vanilla Sponge Cake with Chocolate Mocha Pudding

JAMIE SCHLER
NANTES, FRANCE
LIFE'S A FEAST: CONFESSIONS OF A
GOURMANDE
http://lifesafeast.blogspot.com/2009/07/man-in-moon.html

I'm an American living abroad in a multicultural home with a multicultural kitchen. Baking is my passion, and I love the simple and homey the best. I love cooking, too, but feel that I am still going through the learning process. I love sharing my life stories and experiences as they relate to my baking and cooking. Just like I love learning about others and their lives and experiences, I love inspiring others to start to bake and cook. I am married to a Frenchman, and we have two sons. I am a trained milliner, but have worked in the arts and gastronomy as well.

SERVES 12

Dad, the true engineer, could do it all and do it with help from no one. He was the first to believe in safety belts and solar panels, the first to really talk about garden-grown vegetables and healthy eating, the evils of sugar and smoking. And he baked—baked sheet cakes and marble cakes, Bundt cakes and pudding cakes. Bowls and bowls of pudding topped with Cool Whip. Homemade waffles or huge, light-as-air choux puffs filled with pudding or whipped cream. And amazing prune and apricot compote, the fruit glistening like jewels in the syrupy, just perfectly sweet liquid, plump and tender, bursting in your mouth as you wrapped your tongue around each delicate bite.

My passion for baking grew each time I watched him mix and pour and pop a special treat into the oven, fascinated by the joy and tenderness he exuded with each delicacy he made for us or for friends or for the synagogue's Bingo Night. A quiet, tender, loving man, the same man who, every single night of his life as a father, would take us into his arms, one by one, for a kiss and a hug before we were scooted off to bed. A ritual he never, ever missed.

And on this fortieth anniversary of the moon landing, I send out this note of love to my dad, one of the original twelve research and design engineers of the Space Task Group of the Manned Space Flight Program. He developed the Life Support and Environmental Control Systems for the manned flights from the earliest chimpanzee shot through to the beginnings of the space shuttle design. As the spaceship, each rocket, Mercury, Apollo, or other, was standing proudly on the launch pad, rumbling and seething and raring to go, he would take those few seconds away from Mission Control to call us at home. The phone would ring; someone would pick it up and hear his voice. "Get out in the backyard. Now." And we'd grab the binoculars, and out we would run to watch the takeoff in the

distance, the rocket shooting skyward, its smooth, sleek body roaring heavenward, the stages dropping off, one-two-three, and then we would sigh, the excitement over, and run back into the house to sit in front of the TV and watch the rest until it was out of sight. Then we would return to play or to our books and wait for six o'clock, when he would come back from work for another evening at home.

My dad is now up there in the skies, watching us, and I like to think that I see him smiling down on me each time I stare at the moon, and I shiver and my head spins, and then I turn away and get on with my life.

SPONGE CAKE:

1½ cups all-purpose flour

1 teaspoon baking powder

½ teaspoon salt

6 eggs, separated

1¼ cups sugar

½ cup cold water

2 teaspoons vanilla extract

1 tablespoon amaretto or 1 teaspoon almond extract (optional)

¾ teaspoon cream of tartar or a drop or two of lemon juice and a few grains of salt

CHOCOLATE MOCHA PUDDING:

1 large egg, plus 1 egg yolk

⅓ cup sugar

2 tablespoons cornstarch

2½ cups low-fat milk

1½ tablespoons instant coffee, instant espresso, or coarsely ground coffee beans

Pinch of salt

6 ounces bittersweet or semisweet chocolate (I used 70%), finely chopped

2 teaspoons vanilla extract

Lightly sweetened freshly whipped, cream, for serving

1 Preheat the oven to 325°F. You will need an ungreased 10-inch tube pan.

2 For the sponge cake, blend the flour, baking powder, and salt in a small bowl and set aside.

3 Put the egg yolks in a very large mixing bowl and beat until they turn a pale lemony color. Beat in the sugar and continue beating until very thick. Beat in the dry ingredients in 3 additions, alternating with the water, vanilla, and amaretto. Scrape down the sides as necessary.

4 With perfectly clean beaters, beat the egg whites with the cream of tartar in a clean bowl until stiff peaks form (you should be able to turn the bowl over and they won't budge).

5 Using a spatula, gently fold a quarter to a third of the whites into the cake batter to lighten it. Then gently fold in the rest of the whites in 2 or 3 additions until all the whites are folded in and the batter is well blended (no huge chunks of whites remaining).

6 Carefully pour the batter into the pan. Gently shake the pan back and forth once or twice to make sure the batter is even in the pan, then bake for 55 to 60 minutes, until the top of the cake feels firm like a marshmallow when pressed gently with a finger or two. If it feels or sounds airy or makes a sound like pssssffttt, bake for another couple of minutes. Got it? Cool the cake in the tube pan, inverted on a bottle, for about 15 minutes before turning upright and easing out of the tube pan. Very carefully (it is a delicate cake) slide a thin metal spatula in up-and-down movements all around to loosen the sides, then push the center tube with the cake up and out of the outside ring. Allow to cool completely. Carefully, using the spatula, loosen the bottom and around the tube and have someone else help you flip the cake over onto your two hands. The other person must quickly loosen and lift the center tube up and out, place the serving plate onto the bottom of the cake, and flip it back upright.

7 Meanwhile, make the pudding. In a large, heavy saucepan over medium-high heat, stir together the whole egg, egg yolk, sugar, and cornstarch until thick, smooth, and creamy. Set aside on an unused burner near where you will be heating the milk.

8 In a medium saucepan over medium heat, heat the milk with the coffee and salt. Bring to a gentle boil. Remove the pan from the heat. If you used ground coffee beans, quickly strain the hot milk through a fine sieve. Begin whisking the egg custard without stopping and add a ladleful or two of the hot coffee-milk to the larger saucepan. Add the rest of the hot milk to the egg mixture and whisk. Stir in the finely chopped chocolate until melted and blended.

9 Place this saucepan over medium-high heat and cook, whisking constantly, for 4 to 6 minutes, until the pudding thickens and just starts to boil. Remove the pan from the heat immediately and quickly strain the pudding into a large bowl. Stir in the vanilla.

10 Divide the pudding into 6 pudding bowls. Chill for at least 1 hour before serving. If not serving after this initial chilling, cover with plastic wrap directly on the surface to prevent a skin from forming.

11 Serve with the sponge cake and whipped cream, just like my dad would have done. My dad also made this pudding to fill his choux puffs, which were the size of small coffee cup saucers. Wow!

Oatmaiale Cookies

HILLARY THRASHER
WASHINGTON, DC.
BELLY UP TO THE BLOG
http://bellyuptotheblog.com/blog

I blog in two veins: what's eating me and what I'm eating. Occasionally, when things get really tough, I write about what drives me to drink and what I'm drinking.

MAKES TWENTY-FIVE 3-INCH COOKIES

For a short period when I was a child, Mother sent me to a tennis coach. I don't remember the lessons so much as I remember the breakfast she made me every Saturday morning—oatmeal with brown sugar, raisins, chocolate chips, and milk with a side of bacon (apparently she equated sixty minutes of rec tennis with running the Boston Marathon). Fast-forward thirty years (and slow down my metabolism by as much), and I still crave the concept of this meal but not the pasty texture that seizes into a congealed ball as oatmeal cools. When DC was socked in by a blizzard and I was nostalgic for comfort food, I came up with the idea for this cookie. Granted there's nothing unique about an oatmeal cookie, but an oatmeal cookie with bacon? Now we're cookin'.

CANDIED BACON:

6   strips bacon

1   tablespoon maple syrup

½   cup packed light brown sugar

COOKIE DOUGH:

2½ cups whole-grain rolled oats (not instant)

¾   cup (1½ sticks) unsalted butter, softened but still cool

1   cup granulated sugar

¼   cup packed light brown sugar

1   large egg

1   teaspoon vanilla extract

1   cup unbleached all-purpose flour

¾   teaspoon baking powder

½   teaspoon baking soda

½   teaspoon salt

1   cup dried cherries

¾   cup milk chocolate chips

      Sea salt or finishing salt, preferably Maldon (optional)

1. To make candied bacon, preheat the oven to 350°F and make sure your rack is in the middle position. Line a cookie sheet with parchment. Parcook the bacon in a frying pan to render the fat and pat off excess grease. Mix the maple syrup with the brown sugar and rub to coat the bacon (make sure it's cool enough to handle) with some of it.

2. Place the bacon on the lined cookie sheet, dust with the remaining sugar mixture, and bake for 14 minutes, flipping the bacon half way through the cooking time. Lift the parchment off the cookie sheet and let the bacon cool. When the candied bacon has set up (cool and the sugars have solidified), pulse coarsely in a food processor to obtain bite-sized bits roughly the same size as chocolate chips or raisins.

3. To make the dough, you can toast the oats in a large dry skillet until they are light brown and give off a nutty aroma. Set aside to cool. Or use them untoasted.

4. Using a stand mixer with a paddle attachment, whip the butter with both sugars until fluffy. Add the egg and vanilla and mix until well blended, about 30 seconds.

5. Whisk the flour with the baking powder, baking soda, and salt in a separate bowl. Add the dry ingredients to the beaten butter on low speed until fully incorporated.

6. Gradually add the oats, followed by the candied bacon bits, dried cherries, and milk chocolate chips, just until the ingredients are incorporated throughout the dough.

7. For each cookie, scoop out about 2 tablespoons of cookie dough and roll into a ball; then make a "patty cake" by pressing the dough ball relatively flat between your palms (about ¼ inch thick) and place on a cookie sheet lined with parchment. The cookies will spread a bit, so space them out accordingly. Sprinkle the tops with a few flecks of sea salt.

8. Check the cookies at 12 minutes, but they could bake as long as 15, depending on how you like them. Cool on a wire rack.

Pain Perdu— Brioche French Toast

I love dessert for breakfast! Exactly a year ago, during brunch at Craftbar in Manhattan, we encountered the epitome of perfection that will benchmark all the future French toasts to come. Determined to re-create this recipe at home, I took on the challenge. Bring it on, Tom Colicchio! One of the many reasons why we love Craftbar is that they list French toast as *"pain perdu,"* giving a nod to its origins—translated literally as "lost bread," the ingenuity transpired from an effort to salvage stale bread by soaking it in an eggy mixture.

It was a long year of *pain perdu* experiments in our test kitchen. We knew that Craftbar uses a brioche, and we ducked inside every bakery we passed in search of it. Even our trusted *boulangerie* in Brooklyn, Almondine, failed to showcase this buttery, spongy bread. We settled for an egg challah in the meantime. One day, as I was strolling through SoHo, I passed by Balthazar Bakery. *Mais bien sûr!* How did we manage to overlook such a high-profile *boulangerie*? At long last, we had our beloved brioche loaf. But sadly, the recipe was still not quite right. At Craftbar, the *pain perdu* was perfectly crispy on the outside while the inside was light and fluffy with a hint of sweet custard. And that's when it finally struck me like a bolt of lightning. Custard! The mixture needed to be thick like custard to prevent the bread from getting too soggy. Most recipes require regular milk which bread absorbs far too quickly. And I also decided to omit the egg whites for a truly rich custard mixture. And oh, the sweet taste of victory. I have my genius moments, and this is one of them.

DHALE BAUTISTA
NEW YORK, NEW YORK
CULINARY MUSINGS
http://dhaleb.com/dessert/pain-perdu-the-perfection-of-french-toast

I'm a California girl who received a degree in criminology, law, and society, which oddly led me to a career in event planning, floral design, and as an activities director. I'm also a wanna-be chef who, despite my lack of culinary training, derives expertise from the passion to learn and discover all things food related. Delightfully dorky and amusingly clumsy, I snort when I laugh.

MAKES 6

2　cups heavy whipping cream

½　teaspoon vanilla extract

2　egg yolks

1　tablespoon sugar

　　1-inch-thick slices stale brioche (approximately
　　6 to 12 slices depending on size of loaf)

2　tablespoons butter, melted

1　tablespoon vegetable oil

1 Preheat the oven to 350°F. In a small saucepan, heat the cream with the vanilla. Bring to a slow simmer. Meanwhile, whisk the egg yolks and sugar together in a large bowl until it turns a pale yellow color. Gradually whisk the hot cream into the eggs. Transfer to a shallow dish.

2 Take one slice of bread and dip it into the custard, about 7 seconds on each side. Transfer to a cookie sheet and repeat the process until you have no remaining slices. This works best if your bread is really hard and stale. If your bread is fresh, re-create the right texture by placing your brioche slices in the oven for 5 to 7 minutes.

3 Place a skillet over medium heat. In a small bowl, mix the melted butter and oil. Dip a ball of paper towel into the oil mixture and coat the skillet. One by one, grill each soaked slice of brioche until it is slightly brown, 1 to 2 minutes per side. Transfer back to the cookie sheet. Bake the French toast in the oven for 10 minutes.

TIP: In between grilling slices, use the paper towel to swipe the skillet clean and apply another thin layer of the oil mixture.

JUNO HOUT BAY
CAPE TOWN, SOUTH AFRICA
SCRUMPTIOUS SOUTH AFRICA
http://whatsforsupper-juno.blogspot.com/2010/01/
prickly-pear-granita-and-scorpion.html

I'm forty-seven, a freelance writer, and a mother of three. I've lived in Johannesburg for the past seventeen years and have recently moved to Hout Bay, about half an hour's drive from the centre of Cape Town, South Africa. I've been cooking since I was nine or so, but it's only in the last eleven years that cookery has turned from a hobby (and an often dreary chore) into something of an obsession. I love food, especially simple home cooking that warms your heart and makes your taste buds sing. I don't like cheffy, fiddly, arty-farty food, silly fusions and flavour combinations, food stacked in towers, foams, spooms, smears, dribbles, drizzles, twirly bits, or any recipe that contains the word jus or coulis (unless it's written in French). My cooking/eating style? I love fresh crunchy salads, homemade soups, and all vegetables except butternut and pumpkin. I adore roast meat—beef, lamb, pork, and chicken, in that order—and would like to eat fish every day: fresh, smoked, pickled, or tinned. I have a particular passion for the warming spices of Indian cuisine and am smitten by the combination of pork sausages, mashed potato, and gravy.

SERVES 4

Prickly Pear Granita

I have prickles, spikes, and burny things on my mind today. Last night, my son discovered a large scorpion skulking (with intent, I imagined) in my dog's food bowl. I thought we might see the odd critter in our new garden, tucked up against a mountain, but I hadn't figured on scorpions. I am going to think twice now about walking barefoot in the garden at night. This morning I was alarmed when my husband complained that he was burning and itching all over. Had—shudder—a scorpion burrowed into the bedclothes? Then I remembered that yesterday my daughter (in the interest of science, you understand) had "tested" my canister of pepper spray. I'd laughed it off and told her to wipe up any residue. "What did you clean up the mess with?" I asked. "With dad's bath towel!" she yelled. Finally, scratching in the fridge for breakfast, I found a big bag of prickly pears I'd bought a few days ago and forgotten about. They were the last thing I wanted to touch, feeling as creepy and crawly as I did, but I am just smitten by this most beautiful and refreshing fruit. So I put on a pair of gloves and turned them into a granita. This is a delicate ice with an ethereal flavour, so easy to make and perfect for a hot day.

1   cup sugar

2   cups water

4   prickly pears (cactus pears), chilled

     Juice of 1 lemon

1 Place a large, flat metal dish in the freezer for 2 hours.

2 Put the sugar and water in a saucepan and bring to a boil over high heat. Boil for 5 minutes, stirring occasionally. Remove from the heat and allow to cool completely. Chill.

3 Peel the prickly pears (wear gloves), chop coarsely, and place in a blender. Blend to a thick pulp.

4 Measure the pulp into a bowl. Add the equivalent amount of cooled sugar syrup. Stir in the lemon juice. Pour the mixture into the frozen dish and place in the freezer.

5 After 30 minutes, scratch and scrape the fruit pulp with a fork to form crystals. Continue scraping and scratching every 20 minutes until you have a pile of fluffy, crystalline flakes.

6 Pile the granita into chilled martini glasses and serve immediately.

Pumpkin Latte Crème Brûlée

KARLIE KISER
PLANO, TEXAS
CULINARY CRUMBS
http://www.culinarycrumbs.com/2009/11/pumpkin-latte-creme-brulee.html

I am a burgeoning home cook trying to teach myself new techniques and tricks in the kitchen. I love to bake up something sweet just as much as I love to create rich, savory, and satisfying dishes. Blogging is a new adventure for me, but I am quickly learning that I love so much more about it than just cooking delicious food. Cooking is a continuous learning process. You can never know too much about it!

MAKES 6 CUSTARDS

The arrival of pumpkin spice lattes on the Starbucks menu gets me giddy with anticipation for the upcoming "sweater" weather every year. I had my first of the season a while back, when I was still living in New York, and the tantalizing aromas from the cinnamon and nutmeg combined with the rich espresso got me thinking: wouldn't these flavors make for an excellent dessert? The wheels started churning, and I began to brainstorm the perfect vessel for my pumpkin latte creation. At first I thought cupcakes, perhaps with a pumpkin cake base topped by a mocha buttercream, but that idea didn't leave me too excited. I came up with the idea for a crème brûlée that would marry the flavors of pumpkin pie and a latte into one smooth and silky custard. I am not a very patient person, so I really try my hardest to get a recipe right the first time around. I don't have the time or tenacity (or money) to try a recipe over and over until I get it right. (A personality trait I should probably work on . . .) So I have to say I was thrilled when this recipe came out damn near perfect on my first try. I felt I had achieved the balance of flavors I was looking for, and everything went smoothly (even the texture of the custard) just as I had hoped. At least until I broke out the blowtorch, which was an experience all its own.

1   cup heavy cream

1   cup half-and-half

1   cup pumpkin purée

¼   cup granulated sugar

¼   cup packed light brown sugar

¾   teaspoon cinnamon

¼   teaspoon ground ginger

¼   teaspoon ground cloves

¼   teaspoon freshly grated nutmeg

1   tablespoon espresso powder

6   egg yolks

    Pinch of salt

1   teaspoon vanilla extract

¼   cup turbinado (raw) sugar

1 Preheat the oven to 325°F.

2 In a medium saucepan, whisk together the cream, half-and-half, pumpkin, sugars, spices, and espresso powder.

3 Over medium heat, bring the liquid just to a simmer, or until steam rises. Remove from the heat and set aside.

4 In a large bowl, whisk together the egg yolks and salt. Gradually add the warm cream mixture, whisking to combine. Stir in the vanilla. Strain the custard into a large measuring cup or bowl with a pour spout.

5 Divide the custard evenly among six 6- to 8-ounce ovenproof ramekins. Arrange the filled ramekins in a baking pan, then carefully transfer the pan to the oven. Slowly pour enough hot water into the pan surrounding the ramekins to reach halfway up the sides.

6 Bake the custards until set around the edges but still slightly jiggly (like Jell-O) in the center, 20 to 30 minutes. Let the ramekins rest in the water bath for 5 to 10 minutes. Remove the ramekins and let cool for another 20 minutes. Cover loosely with plastic wrap and chill for at least 6 hours, preferably overnight.

7 When ready to serve, blot the top of the custards dry with a paper towel.

8 Sprinkle 1 teaspoon of turbinado sugar over each ramekin. Using a small kitchen torch, melt the sugar by waving the torch flame 3 to 6 inches from the surface of the sugar. Heat the sugar until it is caramelized and no dry sugar is visible. Sprinkle another teaspoon of turbinado sugar over each custard and continue to caramelize with the kitchen torch until a dark amber crust has formed on top of each custard.

9 Chill the custards for 5 to 10 minutes before serving. Precaramelized custards can be made up to 2 days ahead and chilled until ready to serve.

Rūpjmaizes Kārtojums (Latvian Rye Bread Dessert)

Latvians have some incredibly delicious desserts. A lot of them are made with rye bread, which is an essential part of traditional Latvian cuisine. You can even find rye bread crumb ice cream over here and yogurt with rye bread crumbs. Not to mention cream of bread and bread soup. Even nowadays, as bread is losing its popularity (a lot of people are on a diet and think it's too fattening), public opinion polls say an average Latvian eats up to 50 kg (110 pounds) bread per year. And coarse rye bread is the sort that remains the favourite throughout the years.

This dessert was originally called rūpjmaizes kārtojums, which means "layers of bread." The most common method is to layer rye bread crumbs, whipped cream, and cranberry or cowberry jam. Sometimes creamed cottage cheese is used instead. The dessert can be made in small individual ice cream bowls or in a larger bowl and then cut into portions. We make it in a larger container for four and use mascarpone instead of whipped cream. Imagine rye bread crumbs toasted with sugar and cinnamon, layered with tangy mashed cranberries, and topped with soft, vanilla-flavoured mascarpone; repeat once and top with those crunchy bread crumbs. Sounds good, uh? Fresh cranberries can be replaced with sour cranberry jam if you prefer.

ALINA PETROPAVLOVSKA
RIGA, LATVIA
RUSSIAN SEASON
http://www.russianseason.net/index.php/2009/12/
rupjmaizes-kartojums-layered-latvian-rye-bread-dessert

Did you ever want to know more about Eastern European cuisine? Russian Season is a food blog run by two Russian-speaking women—a mother (Natalia) and a daughter (Alina) living in Latvia. We cook most of the dishes together, while Alina writes the posts. We share some (tweaked and adapted) recipes from Russia, Eastern Europe, and the former USSR with our readers.

SERVES 4

10 slices coarse rye bread, slightly
    dried and crust removed

¼   cup sugar

1   tablespoon ground cinnamon

8   ounces mascarpone cheese

3   tablespoons heavy cream

½   teaspoon vanilla sugar

6   tablespoons cranberries mashed
    with 2 tablespoons sugar

1   Grate the slices of bread on a hand grater.

2   Preheat the oven to 350°F. In a 13 by 9-inch nonstick pan, mix the breadcrumbs, 2 tablespoons of the sugar, and the cinnamon. Toast in the oven for 20 minutes, stirring and breaking up any lumps with a spatula. Leave to cool.

3   Combine the mascarpone cheese, remaining 2 tablespoons sugar, cream, and vanilla sugar in a medium bowl. Stir well. Divide the mascarpone mixture into two parts.

4   Divide the toasted breadcrumbs into 3 parts, two equal and one slightly smaller (we'll use it for topping).

5   Put one of the equal parts of breadcrumbs on the bottoms of 4 small ice cream bowls. With a spatula or spoon, divide half the mascarpone mixture between the dishes, and gently spread. Divide 3 tablespoons of mashed cranberries over the mascarpone mixture. Repeat with another layer of bread, mascarpone, and cranberries. Cover the dishes and set them in the fridge. Chill the dessert for 5 to 10 hours.

6   Top each dish with a thinner layer of the remaining bread crumbs and serve.

Spicy Pumpkin Carrot Muffins

CHRISTIE MORGAN ISON
LITTLE ROCK, ARKANSAS
FANCY PANTS FOODIE
http://arfoodie.wordpress.com/2009/10/05/spicy-pumpkin-carrot-muffins

I'm a budding culinarian (that's a fun word, huh?) with a background in marketing and public relations. I began culinary school in January 2010 and am blogging through the process. My blog also focuses on from-scratch, nonprocessed-food (as much as possible) home cooking, as well as the food scene in Arkansas. I like to highlight chefs, food events, trends, and more in the area and would eventually like to "franchise" writing of these topics to other metro areas for the site.

MAKES 28 MUFFINS

Today is my mom's birthday. Mom didn't want a supersweet cake, so I decided to make something seasonal and just sorta sweet. I started reading through various cookbooks' versions of pumpkin bread, pumpkin cake, pumpkin muffins. Muffins seemed my best bet, but the recipes were making me yawn. So I put on my Fancy Pants hat and got creative. Hence the following recipe.

Whenever I cook with my daughter, I tell her, whenever possible, to use a "secret" or "surprise" ingredient, something that nobody would try or find it easy to pick out exactly what "that something" might be. She was at school today while I made the muffins, but I think she would have gone in the same direction. Cayenne. And baby food. Don't be afraid. It really is yummy.

In my original batch, I put the cayenne on only three of the muffins, as an experiment. I should have done them all! Well, kids probably wouldn't like it, so maybe you could go half and half. They smell incredible, aren't too sweet, and have a great depth of flavor, even without the cayenne. The carrot purée keeps the whole thing moist. And you don't have to tell anyone it's baby food or even that it has carrots at all.

1   14-ounce can puréed pumpkin or 1¾ cups of puréed cooked pumpkin

1   cup (2 sticks) unsalted butter, at room temperature

⅔   cup unsulphured molasses

2   cups packed dark brown sugar

2   eggs, beaten, at room temperature

1   3½-ounce jar carrot baby food or ½ cup of puréed cooked carrot

3½ cups all-purpose flour

½   teaspoon salt

2   teaspoons baking soda

3   teaspoons ground cinnamon

2   teaspoons freshly grated nutmeg

½   cup dried cranberries, raisins, or currants

¼   cup almond slivers, walnut halves or pieces, or pecan halves or pieces

⅛   teaspoon ground dried chipotle or cayenne (smoked if you have it)

1   Preheat the oven to 400°F. Line standard-size muffin cups with paper liners. If using fresh pumpkin, strain the purée for at least 30 minutes in cheesecloth or a wire sieve.

2   In a stand mixer, cream the butter at medium-high speed until soft and lightened in color. Add the molasses and 1½ cups of the brown sugar, beating until combined and light in texture.

3   Add the eggs, pumpkin, and puréed carrot and mix on medium speed until blended.

4   In a separate bowl or on a flexible cutting board, sift together the flour, salt, baking soda, cinnamon, and nutmeg. Pour into the wet ingredients and gently fold the ingredients together, being careful not to overmix.

5   Fold in the cranberries, raisins, or currants.

6   Using a spoon or large scoop (what I used), fill the muffin cups three-quarters full. Place three almond slivers in the middle of each muffin top, pointing up slightly in a radiating pattern. (If using walnut or pecan halves, place one at an upward angle in the middle of each muffin. If using pieces, sprinkle a small amount on each muffin.)

7   In a small bowl, mix the remaining ½ cup brown sugar with the chipotle or cayenne powder. Sprinkle liberally on top of the muffins. Bake for 12 to 15 minutes. Best if served immediately so the topping remains crisp.

Swirled Chocolate Bark

JOANNE AND ADAM
OLD TOWN ALEXANDRIA, VIRGINIA
INSPIRED TASTE
http://www.inspiredtaste.net/recipes/swirled-chocolate-bark

My name is Joanne. My husband, Adam, and I work on the website as a couple who love food, cooking, and each other.

MAKES 18 TO 20 PIECES

Can you believe how close we are to the end of the year? We certainly can't. Every year Adam and I plan to get presents early, decorate, and plan how to fit in all those holiday parties and get-togethers with friends and family, but then every year we are behind on presents, have no clue how to fit in seeing everyone before the holidays, and still have a Halloween wreath hanging on our front door! To be fair, this year we have done a little better. We do still have the Halloween wreath up on our door, but we have put up AND decorated our Christmas tree and have planned, purchased, but not wrapped about half the amount of presents we would like to get. We have also started to get excited about the food and drinks. You know, the "I have been on a diet for the last month so I can eat all I want during the holidays" food and drink, although to be honest, we have not been on a diet for the past month, but will still probably end up eating all we want anyway. But hey, I guess that is what a New Year's resolution is for, right?

A couple of days ago, feeling in the holiday mood, we decided to make some festive candy. One of the easiest, cheapest, prettiest, and tastiest holiday candies is chocolate bark. It's so simple yet has just the right touch of elegance. The possibilities are endless. You could use whatever type of chocolate you like best (white, milk, dark, a combination of all three), you can top it with just about anything you think would taste good with chocolate (candy cane, nuts, dried fruit, your favorite store-bought candy, pretzels), and people always love it.

For our version we wanted to go festive, so we swirled melted white and semisweet chocolate infused with orange zest, then topped it with bright green pistachios and bright red dried cranberries. It looks fabulous and tastes great. You could easily wrap some up in some pretty cellophane bags or arrange some in a nice box for a host or hostess gift or even serve it alongside some coffee at the end of a nice meal. The process for making chocolate bark is pretty simple and won't take too

¼ cup shelled pistachios in halves or roughly chopped

8 ounces semisweet chocolate (either chocolate chips or a chocolate bar broken into small pieces)

6 ounces white chocolate (either chocolate chips or a chocolate bar broken into small pieces)

1 tablespoon grated orange zest, plus a little for sprinkling on top

¼ cup roughly chopped dried cranberries

much time, probably about 20 minutes. Then, you just have to wait about 2 hours for the chocolate to firm up before you can break it into pieces for serving.

1 In a dry skillet, lightly toast the pistachios, then set aside to cool.

2 Line a 9 by 10-inch cookie sheet with parchment and set aside.

3 Melt the semisweet and white chocolate simultaneously in separate double boilers or one at a time in the microwave (in a medium microwave-safe bowl, microwave the chocolate until melted, stirring every 30 seconds to prevent overheating). While the semisweet chocolate melts, add a tablespoon of orange zest.

4 Once both chocolates are melted, pour the semisweet chocolate onto the prepared baking sheet and smooth it out into a rectangle. Drop spoonfuls of the melted white chocolate on top. Use a wooden skewer or the tip of a knife to swirl the chocolates together until you are happy with the swirled design.

5 Sprinkle the pistachios and cranberries over the swirled chocolate, then sprinkle a little more orange zest on top. Cool at room temperature for approximately 2 hours, or until the chocolate is hard and can be broken or cut into pieces. Break or cut the chocolate bark into 1 by 3-inch pieces and serve at room temperature.

The Color Purple Yam Dessert

MIKA ONO
SAN DIEGO, CALIFORNIA
ANCIENT WISDOM, MODERN KITCHEN
http://ancientwisdommodernkitchen.blogspot.
com/2010/01/color-purple-yam-dessert-recipe.html

I am the author of *Ancient Wisdom, Modern Kitchen: Recipes for Health, Healing, and Long Life* (Da Capo Lifelong Books, March 2010) with Dr. Yuan Wang, L.Ac., and Warren Sheir, L.Ac. I live in southern California with my family.

MAKES ABOUT 12 PIECES, SERVING 6

The Chinese mountain yam *(Dioscorea opposita)* is a key herb in traditional Chinese medicine. Although unassumingly tan-brown on the outside, once you cut it open, you can see the inside is a vibrant purple. The purple yam is featured in Philippine sweet desserts, Vietnamese soups, Indian dishes, and Hawaiian cuisine, as well as Chinese recipes. This Chinese recipe using purple yam blends the smooth texture of the yam with sweet rice flour, accented with a sweet, nutty filling. The dessert also happens to be wheat-free, dairy-free, and vegan. We found purple yams at a local Asian supermarket.

According to traditional Chinese medicine, the basic yam recipe is good for counteracting general weakness, fatigue, lack of appetite, and constipation. Goji berries help the vision, and walnuts are believed to contribute to longevity. For those familiar with the language of traditional Chinese medicine, the purple yam strengthens the spleen *qi* and counteracts blood stasis. With goji berries, this dessert helps to nourish the blood and the yin, increase the essence, and improve vision; with walnuts, it helps strengthen the kidneys, warm the lungs, and moisten the intestines.

Any dried fruit can be substituted for the goji berries. Dried apples, for example, are lovely. Also, other seeds or nuts, such as pumpkin seeds, chopped almonds, black sesame seeds, pine nuts, or chopped peanuts, offer possibilities instead of walnuts.

1　medium purple yam (about 1 pound), peeled and cut into 2-inch pieces

¾　cup sweet rice flour (also known as sticky rice flour or glutinous rice flour)

½　cup raw unsalted walnuts, finely chopped

2　tablespoons goji berries

1　tablespoon honey or barley malt

1 to 2 tablespoons vegetable oil, such as olive or canola

1 Steam or boil the pieces of purple yam for about 15 minutes, until soft. Allow the yam to cool for a few minutes, then transfer it to a mixing bowl and mash it with a fork until smooth.

2 Gradually add the sweet rice flour to the yam, kneading the mixture together with your hands to form a smooth dough. (If the dough starts to get too crumbly, stop adding the rice flour; if you have already overdone it, you can compensate by adding a little water.)

3 Combine the chopped walnuts, goji berries, and honey (warm the honey first if it is too solid to mix easily) in a small bowl.

4 Make a cup out of a piece of dough, fill it with the fruit and nut stuffing, and close the dough around it to make a ball.

5 Flatten the ball with the palms of your hands to form it into a 3-inch round pancake shape.

6 Repeat until the dough and the filling is used up, making about 12 pieces.

7 Heat a skillet over a medium-high heat. Add the oil, then cook the pieces until both sides are brown and the center is warm, 5 to 10 minutes. Cook in batches if necessary. Serve warm.

Triple Citrus Cake

THE DUO DISHES
LOS ANGELES, CALIFORNIA
THE DUO DISHES
http://duodishes.com/2009/04/03/citrus-is-our-new-black

We are Chrystal and Amir, two people who love to cook, love to eat, and love to talk about cooking and eating. We live in Los Angeles, which is of course where we spend so much time doing all of that cooking and eating. With no formal culinary training, our prowess in the kitchen is led primarily by our internal yum factor. We create new recipes, eyeball measurements, and taste until it's perfect. Or at least pretty close.

SERVES 10

How easy is it to pick out your favorite ingredient? We're going to cheat and use one word that really encompasses several complementary, yet unique ingredients–citrus. On our blog, if you go to the search bar, type in lemon, lime, orange, or zest, a million of our recipes should pop up. Citrus fruit flavors are always so clean and fresh, they accentuate other ingredients, and they can add great color to a dish. There's nothing better than popping it into a recipe for extra yet subtle oomph. This is a very basic yogurt cake—with a few tweaks, shall we say. It is supermoist and terribly delectable. We used a combination of lime yogurt, lemon zest, and orange juice. Of course you could test several other permutations. If Bobby Brown could live by his own prerogative, then why not you?

TRIPLE CITRUS CAKE:

1½ cups all-purpose flour

2   teaspoons baking powder

½   teaspoon salt

1   cup lime yogurt

4   eggs

¾   cup sugar

1   teaspoon vanilla extract

½   cup grapeseed oil

    Zest of 2 lemons, minced

GLAZE:

1   cup confectioners' sugar

2   tablespoons orange juice

1 Preheat the oven to 350°F. Coat a 9 by 5-inch loaf pan with floured baking spray (or use parchment paper coated with baking spray as well).

2 Whisk the flour, baking powder, and salt together in a medium bowl. Set aside.

3 With an electric mixer, beat the yogurt, eggs, sugar, vanilla, oil, and lemon zest in a large bowl until combined. Switch to a spatula and fold in the dry ingredients until incorporated.

4 Pour the batter into the prepared pan and smooth evenly. Bake for 40 to 50 minutes, or until a cake tester comes out clean.

5 Allow the cake to cool at least an hour.

6 When the cake is cool, remove the pan and place on a serving plate or cake platter. Mix the confectioners' sugar with orange juice in a medium bowl until smooth and drizzle the glaze over the cake.

Wild Blackberry Sorbet with Garden Mint and Lavender

EVE FOX
BERKELEY, CALIFORNIA
THE GARDEN OF EATING
http://gardenofeatingblog.blogspot.com/2008/07/
wild-blackberry-sorbet-with-garden-mint.html

I live in Berkeley, California, where I tend my blog about food—the growing, producing, procuring, cooking, and eating of it. I have a legendary love of aprons and can often be found squeezing fruits and veggies at one of the many local farmers' markets.

SERVES 4

I grew up in the lush countryside of New York's Hudson River valley. As a little girl, picking the wild blackberries that grew down the street from my house was one of my favorite things to do in the hot, hazy days of late summer. My friend Emily and I would wander down the road from my house, stopping every few feet to pop the black bubbles of tar that had formed in the heat. When we finally reached the bramble, we'd steel ourselves for a moment, then plunge into the thick patch of blackberry canes, doing our best to avoid the thorns. The berries were abundant—there were always plenty to take home even after stuffing ourselves.

Picking blackberries was one of the sacred rituals of summertime. Unfortunately, in the decades since I left home my life as a city dweller has not offered me many opportunities to pick berries. So I was delighted to discover upon moving to the East Bay a few years ago that blackberries flourish in many parts of this urban environment. Yesterday we joined our good friends for a picking expedition in their Oakland hills neighborhood. The steep, dry hillsides are covered in blackberries—the canes seem to favor the rarely used public stairways that provide a shortcut through the hills. We started out with clean hands and empty buckets and worked our way through the neighborhood, relieving the canes of their ripe berries as we went. We picked in peace with only a few curious and amused glances from passing drivers and returned an hour later with our hands stained purple, our arms scratched, and our buckets brimming with blackberries.

Back at the house, we washed the berries carefully to remove the dust and dislodge the little bugs we'd carried home. When they'd drained, we laid the berries out singly on cookie sheets— by far the easiest way to prepare them for freezing. Once they are frozen, you can use a metal spatula to simply scoop them off the tray into a resealable plastic bag or other container and then pop them back in the freezer to be used for smoothies, sauces, etc., whenever you want them.

My husband had made a simple yet delicious blackberry sorbet after similar picking expeditions last summer, and we were eager to make our first batch of the season. But this time I decided it would be fun to experiment with adding some fresh herbs from our garden—mint and lavender. The wild blackberry sorbet was a breathtakingly beautiful purple (J. Crew's colorists might call it either "burgundy" or "cabernet") and the taste was no less breathtaking—cool and smooth, sweet yet tart, with subtle notes of lavender and mint. The simple recipe follows. Feel free to make slight adjustments to taste.

3 cups fresh blackberries, washed and dried

¼ cup water

¼ cup organic sugar

1 handful of fresh mint leaves, washed and dried

3 sprigs fresh lavender, washed and dried

1. Lay the clean, drained berries in a single layer on a cookie sheet and place in the freezer until frozen through. It is best to do both this and the next step the day or night before you plan to make the sorbet. The berries need enough time to freeze solid.

2. Make the herb-infused simple syrup by combining the water, sugar, and herbs in a small heavy-bottomed saucepan. Heat over medium heat until it comes to a boil. Take the saucepan off the heat and let cool completely.

3. Strain out the mint leaves and lavender and pour the cooled syrup into an ice cube tray. You should get roughly 4 syrup cubes. Place the tray in the freezer until the syrup is frozen (the cubes may remain a little mushy as a result of all the sugar).

4. Once the berries and herb-infused syrup cubes have frozen, you can make the sorbet. Place the frozen berries and syrup cubes in a food processor or blender and add a few teaspoons of ice water to aid in blending. Continue to process or blend, adding small amounts of the ice water as needed, until smooth.

5. Serve, topped with a sprig of mint leaves and/or lavender.

The Ultimate Dessert

AMANDA SHAFER
MINNESOTA
I AM BAKER
http://iammommy.typepad.com/i_am_
baker/2010/01/the-ultimate-dessert.html

I am a baker: confections, creations, and lots and lots
of calories.

SERVES 12

CINNAMON CRISPS:

¾ cup (1½ sticks) butter at room temperature

1 cup granulated sugar

1 egg

1½ cups all-purpose flour

1 tablespoon ground cinnamon

FILLING:

8 tablespoons (1 stick) unsalted butter, softened

3 cups confectioners' sugar

¼ cup milk

1 teaspoon vanilla extract

½ teaspoon almond extract

TOPPING:

Hot fudge or milk chocolate, melted

This is a cinnamon sugar cookie with frosting and hot fudge drizzle. I made this ultimate dessert with a wonderfully rich vanilla frosting. I have no idea what I was thinking. It's almost too sweet. Even for me. However, right after hubby ate one, he asked me, "What was that?" I explained it to him in great detail, and he just sat there looking at me. Uh-oh. Then he said, "That was by far the best thing I have ever tasted in my whole life. Better than any cake or cookie or cheesecake. Amazing." That is a big compliment from my non-sweet-liking husband. I think I WILL be trying this again.

1 Preheat the oven to 375°F. Place a Silpat sheet or parchment paper on a baking pan.

2 To make the cinnamon crisps, combine the butter and sugar in a large bowl. Beat with an electric mixer until light and fluffy. Add the egg and incorporate well. Add the flour and cinnamon and mix until combined.

3 For each cookie, form a full tablespoon of dough into a ball and place on the Silpat or paper. Flour your hands and press down until the dough is about ⅛ inch thick. Bake for 6 to 8 minutes, until light brown.

4 For the filling, place the butter in a large mixing bowl. Add 1 cup of the confectioners' sugar, the milk, and the vanilla and almond extracts. On medium speed with an electric mixer, beat until smooth and creamy, 3 to 5 minutes. Gradually add the remaining confectioners' sugar, 1 cup at a time, beating well after each addition. This will take about 2 minutes, and you may not need all the sugar. You want a thick pancake batter consistency. Add milk to water it down if needed, sugar to thicken.

5 After the cookies have cooled, you can assemble the sandwiches. For each sandwich, take one cookie and place it on your plate or serving tray. Gently add the filling, using a piping bag. Add another cookie, then another layer of filling. Gently add another cookie to the top. Drizzle the top and sides with hot fudge or melted milk chocolate.

Blog Roll

100 MILES, 74–75
Charles G. Thompson

A TASTE OF SAVOIE, 28
Sarah

A CONSCIOUS FEAST, 70–71
Nicole Aloni

A YANKEE IN A SOUTHERN KITCHEN, 18–19
Kim Morgan

A DOCTOR'S KITCHEN: RECIPE OF THE WEEK AND ODDS & ENDS, 112–113
Deborah Chud

ACTIVE FOODIE, 40–41
Active Foodie

A MEASURED MEMORY, 139–141
Martha Miller

AMATEUR GOURMAND, 72–73
Jenn Davis

A SLICE OF EARTHLY DELIGHT, 114–115
Maya Rook

ANCIENT WISDOM, MODERN KITCHEN, 178–179
Mika Ono

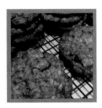

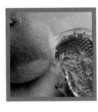

KO RASOI, 94–95
Sanjana Modha

LA TAVOLA MARCHE, 80–81
Ashley and Jason Bartner

LES PETITES GOURMETTES, 16–17
Linda Hopkins

LICK MY SPOON, 152
Stephanie Im

LIFE'S A FEAST: CONFESSIONS OF A GOURMANDE, 161–163
Jamie Schler

MARRIED TO CHOCOLATE, 160
Kris Alcantara

MOMOFUKU FOR 2, 96–97
Momofukufor2

MY COOKING HUT, 104–105
My Cooking Hut

MY DELICIOUS BLOG, 6
Joe Damrongphiwat

MY MAN'S BELLY, 134–135
Pamela

NOTES FROM MY FOOD DIARY, 150–151
Eliza Adam

PEAS LOVE CARROTS, 106–107
Mathea Tanner

PIACERE—FOOD & TRAVEL WITHOUT RULES!, 136–137
Patricia Turo Klosters

SEATTLE FOOD GEEK, 24–25
Scott Heimendinger

POTATO CHOPS AND BONELESS CHICKEN, 116–117
Beverley Ann D'Cruz

SENSE AND SERENDIPITY, 36–37
Divina

PURPLE HOUSE DIRT, 14
Jenny Richards

SHE BREWS GOOD ALE, 61–63
Marika Josephson

RUSSIAN SEASON, 172–173
Alina Petropavlovska

SKIP TO MALOU, 92–93
Skip to Malou

SAVOUR FARE, 122–123
Kate

SPICIE FOODIE, 90–91
Nancy

SCRUMPTIOUS SOUTH AFRICA, 168–169
Juno Hout Bay

SPRINKLE BAKES, 142–143
Sprinklebakes

STUFF TO EAT, 156–157
Lori Jablons

SWEET KAROLINE, 118–119
Karoline Boehm-Goodnick

TALK OF TOMATOES, 15
Janelle

TASTE BUDDIES, 132–133
Syrie Wongkaew

TASTEFOOD, 76–77
Lynda Balslev

TASTY EATS AT HOME, 58
Alta

THE BAKING BEAUTIES, 111
Jeanine Friesen

THE CHEF IN MY HEAD, 44–45
The Chef In My Head

THE DOG'S BREAKFAST, 86–87
David Rollins

THE DUO DISHES, 180–181
The Duo Dishes

**THE GARDEN OF EATING,
182–183**
Eve Fox

THE KICHEN OF OZ, 46–47
Ozhan Ozturk

THE MODERN GASTRONOMER, 52–53
Christopher Testani

THE WINTER GUEST: THE WORLD SEEN FROM MY KITCHEN, 120–121
Miriam

THE ROYAL KITCHEN, 99
Rena Wasser and Tom Sperber

TOKYO TERRACE, 12–13
Rachael White

THE RUNAWAY SPOON, 128–129
The Runaway Spoon

TOKYO TERRACE, 88–89
Brad White

THE SUITCASE CHEF, 126–127
Brittan Heller

TRAMIE'S KITCHEN, 158
Tramie

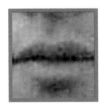

THE ULTERIOR EPICURE, 153–155
Ulterior Epicure

VEGAN VISITOR, 32–33
Dayna McIsaac

THE WICKED (AWESOME) WHISK, 48–49
Marc and Kelly Marino

VEGETARIAN IN ME, 7
Rajani

Metric Conversions and Equivalents

APPROXIMATE METRIC EQUIVALENTS

Volume

¼ teaspoon	1 milliliter
½ teaspoon	2.5 milliliters
¾ teaspoon	4 milliliters
1 teaspoon	5 milliliters
1¼ teaspoons	6 milliliters
1½ teaspoons	7.5 milliliters
1¾ teaspoons	8.5 milliliters
2 teaspoons	10 milliliters
1 tablespoon (½ fluid ounce)	15 milliliters
2 tablespoons (1 fluid ounce)	30 milliliters
¼ cup	60 milliliters
⅓ cup	80 milliliters
½ cup (4 fluid ounces)	120 milliliters
⅔ cup	160 milliliters
¾ cup	180 milliliters
1 cup (8 fluid ounces)	240 milliliters
1¼ cups	300 milliliters
1½ cups (12 fluid ounces)	360 milliliters
1⅔ cups	400 milliliters
2 cups (1 pint)	460 milliliters
3 cups	700 milliliters
4 cups (1 quart)	0.95 liter
1 quart plus ¼ cup	1 liter
4 quarts (1 gallon)	3.8 liters

Weight

¼ ounce	7 grams
½ ounce	14 grams
¾ ounce	21 grams
1 ounce	28 grams
1¼ ounces	35 grams
1½ ounces	42.5 grams
1⅔ ounces	45 grams
2 ounces	57 grams
3 ounces	85 grams
4 ounces (¼ pound)	113 grams
5 ounces	142 grams
6 ounces	170 grams
7 ounces	198 grams
8 ounces (½ pound)	227 grams
16 ounces (1 pound)	454 grams
35.25 ounces (2.2 pounds)	1 kilogram

Length

⅛ inch	3 millimeters
¼ inch	6 millimeters
½ inch	1¼ centimeters
1 inch	2½ centimeters
2 inches	5 centimeters
2½ inches	6 centimeters
4 inches	10 centimeters
5 inches	13 centimeters
6 inches	15¼ centimeters
12 inches (1 foot)	30 centimeters

METRIC CONVERSION FORMULAS

To Convert	Multiply
Ounces to grams	Ounces by 28.35
Pounds to kilograms	Pounds by .454
Teaspoons to milliliters	Teaspoons by 4.93
Tablespoons to milliliters	Tablespoons by 14.79
Fluid ounces to milliliters	Fluid ounces by 29.57
Cups to milliliters	Cups by 236.59
Cups to liters	Cups by .236
Pints to liters	Pints by .473
Quarts to liters	Quarts by .946
Gallons to liters	Gallons by 3.785
Inches to centimeters	Inches by 2.54

OVEN TEMPERATURES

To convert Fahrenheit to Celsius, subtract 32 from Fahrenheit, multiply the result by 5, then divide by 9.

Description	Fahrenheit	Celsius	British Gas Mark
Very cool	200°	95°	0
Very cool	225°	110°	¼
Very cool	250°	120°	½
Cool	275°	135°	1
Cool	300°	150°	2
Warm	325°	165°	3
Moderate	350°	175°	4
Moderately hot	375°	190°	5
Fairly hot	400°	200°	6
Hot	425°	220°	7
Very hot	450°	230°	8
Very hot	475°	245°	9

COMMON INGREDIENTS AND THEIR APPROXIMATE EQUIVALENTS

1 cup uncooked white rice = 185 grams

1 cup all-purpose flour = 140 grams

1 stick butter (4 ounces · ½ cup · 8 tablespoons) = 110 grams

1 cup butter (8 ounces · 2 sticks · 16 tablespoons) = 220 grams

1 cup brown sugar, firmly packed = 225 grams

1 cup granulated sugar = 200 grams

Information compiled from a variety of sources, including *Recipes into Type* by Joan Whitman and Dolores Simon (Newton, MA: Biscuit Books, 2000); *The New Food Lover's Companion* by Sharon Tyler Herbst (Hauppauge, NY: Barron's, 1995); and *Rosemary Brown's Big Kitchen Instruction Book* (Kansas City, MO: Andrews McMeel, 1998).

Index